ESCAPE FROM THE SOVIETS

THE AUTHOR'S SON, ANDREY

(see note on p. 5)

ESCAPE FROM THE SOVIETS

BY

TATIANA TCHERNAVIN

Translated from the Russian by

N. ALEXANDER

NEW YORK
E. P. DUTTON & CO., INC.
1934

.

PUBLISHERS' NOTE

WE are unable to reproduce photographs of the author or her husband as they fear that this might enable the OGPU agents in Finland to trace them.

CONTENTS

PART ONE

CONTENTS—*Continued*

PREFACE

THIS book is about myself, for I cannot write of other people without exposing them to the danger of imprisonment and exile; but my life is typical of the lives of thousands of educated women in U.S.S.R.

We have all of us spent years in study in order to acquire knowledge necessary not only to ourselves but to our country which we were eager to serve. None of us were hostile to the Revolution, and many devoted themselves with enthusiasm to work for the new regime. But this did not save us either from famine, when we had no food to give our children, or from prison and exile.

If technical experts who created all that may be truly called 'achievements of the Revolution' have been condemned by the Soviet Government as 'wreckers' it was but natural that the 'wreckers' wives' should suffer too. To wipe out the intellectuals as a class it was necessary to get hold not only of the men but of the women as well, and, incidentally, of their children.

The campaign of terrorism which began three years ago is not over yet. I do not know who may survive it; but for the sake of friends who are still alive and of the dear ones killed by the OGPU, I want to tell the sad truth about our life in Soviet Russia.

TATIANA TCHERNAVIN.

Finland, 1933.

9

·

ESCAPE FROM THE SOVIETS

PART ONE

CHAPTER I

THE BIRTH OF MY SON

MY son was born on the last warm day of September, 1918. Red and yellow leaves rustled in the garden in the soft sunlight, the sky was blue – all was as it should be in a fine autumn.

That was the first year of the Bolshevik rule; life was getting more and more disorganised; famine was threatening. All were talking of it, but no one understood as yet how terrible it was going to be.

The Revolution as such did not frighten me; I was brought up in a very liberal professorial family and felt convinced that the overthrow of the autocracy would lead to real political freedom. We were not afraid of material difficulties; I thought that under any conditions my husband and I, both well qualified and hardworking people, could be certain of earning a living. But the first sensation I felt on waking up on the morning after my son was born was hunger. I was positively ashamed of the way it forced itself upon my mind.

We had practically no money left: we could just

manage to pay the doctor. I was to have been paid for some literary work, but the publisher had to wind up his business suddenly and I never received my fee.

My husband took on another job in addition to his· work at the University, I returned to my teaching, but prices of food-stuffs were soaring, and our joint monthly salaries were not enough to keep us for a fortnight. I was given as much food as could be spared, but it was fearfully little! I did not dare confess even to myself how I suffered from hunger, especially after nursing the baby. My head reeled, my back ached, I felt so weak' that I could have given anything for some really nourishing food. But in those days we could get nothing except the daily ration of half a pound of black bread, a microscopic quantity of butter to put into the soup and a few mangel-wurzels and turnips; potatoes were a rarity. Meat and fish were an inaccessible luxury. I had never imagined in the old days that food could be such a problem!

It frightened me to look at my husband: he was getting thinner at an incredible rate. His face looked transparent, his eyes were feverish. He had abscesses on his hands from underfeeding.

In those days we often avoided each other. Meals were particularly trying: we were both hungry, and neither could make the other eat. It was a mere pretence at eating, like a meal on the stage when actors rattle forks and knives on empty plates to give the illusion of a sumptuous dinner.

And the baby screamed and could never wait in patience for his next feed. He was rosy and his eyes were azure-blue, but his stomach was drawn in like that of a borzoi pup, and he cried so much that we had to call in a doctor.

Doctors are often excellent people, but they have a dreadful habit of speaking about things which everyone avoids mentioning and of making impossible demands.

'Your baby is perfectly well, but he is hungry,' said the doctor.

'What am I to do?' I asked mechanically.

'Give him more food.'

We said nothing, feeling utterly crushed.

'Where do you teach?' the doctor asked me sternly.

'At the Commercial School.'

'How many hours ?'

'Six hours a day.'

'Why so much?'

'Four hours lessons, two hours compulsory "social work".'

'How do you manage to nurse the baby, then?'

'I teach from nine till eleven, run home to nurse him, return to the school and teach from one till three, then home again, and go back to work from six till eight.'

'How long does the journey take you?'

'Twenty minutes if I walk very fast.'

'Six times a day twenty minutes' walk – that's two hours, plus six hours work. You can't do that and nurse the baby. You must put him on a bottle. There's nothing else I can tell you. The Government is opening now special Infant Welfare Centres. If you can prove that you are poor, you can get milk from there for the baby, but I warn you that their milk is bad: there's too much oatmeal water added to it.'

The doctor told me how much milk I ought to give baby, how to dilute it, and so on, and went away.

Left alone, we could not look each other in the eyes. What had we done! We had brought a child into the world and now could not feed it. We both worked from morning till night, and yet our child was crying with hunger.

'I will try to get one more job,' my husband said. 'They say that at the Agronomical Institute they give the professors a bottle of milk a day. Two academicians have accepted work there. You see, the Imperial dairy farm at Tsarskoe Selo is theirs now.'

'But are there any vacancies on the staff?'

'I believe there are. I'll go and see the Director to-morrow.'

The following day was Sunday. My husband went to Tsarskoe, and I decided to spend the day in bed, hoping that rest would do me good and I should have more milk.

It was pouring with rain. The rooms were cold and damp, but the baby was warm in his Japanese basket, and I wrapped myself up in a shawl and lay quite still. I felt very sad.

Here was a new creature come into the world; its existence was so simple: when it had had enough to eat, it slept; when it was hungry it opened its eyes and mouth and cried till it was fed. But there was not enough food, and no chance of getting any, though it was only a question of half a pint of milk a day.

Round the town were villages where there were cows and milk, but special police at the railway stations took the milk away from the peasant women who brought it to the town, so as to force them to sell it to the Government organisations for worthless paper money. If one went to the villages to buy food, the peasants asked in exchange anything they fancied – clothes, pillows, blankets, watches, pictures, even pianos. I had nothing to offer them because we had just started housekeeping and were short of everything. We had only four chairs in our three rooms!

What should we do if my husband had no luck at Tsarskoe? I lay there, thinking, and reading over my mother's letter. 'We are as badly off for food as you are,' she wrote. 'Your sister is so busy that she leaves home at nine and sometimes does not return till eleven at night. She has charge of two laboratories, lectures at two University Schools and does practical work. I have learnt to cook "with nothing" and she says it is very nice, but I am afraid she is badly underfed. There's nothing but boiled grain and soup with a little cereal and potato in it. A pound of butter has to last us a month, and a pound of sugar also; we hardly ever get two pounds of sugar a month. I take tea with saccharine so as to leave sugar to her. I write "tea" from habit – it's dirty-coloured liquid made with baked oats. I am very uneasy about you and the baby. Try to sell something. The wife of Professor E. takes things on commission and sells them in the street. He lectures in five or six University Schools, but that's not enough to feed their family.'

How ridiculous it all seemed! How long could one go on like this?

The day dragged slowly on; I could not do anything till the question of milk was settled.

It was dusk when my husband came back. I lay still

and listened intently: he opened the door and shut it quietly, with a steady hand. He took off his things quickly and walked up the passage with a firm tread. Could it mean good news? Yes, he came in looking cheerful and excited.

'Well?'

'I am going to lecture at the Agronomical Institute and take charge of the Zoological laboratory. They will give me a pint of milk a day.'

I still remember the feeling of glowing warmth at my heart when I heard this. The child was saved.

His father stood bending over the cot.

'I'll give you the bottle myself to-morrow, puppy. Your daddy's science has come in useful, after all.'

CHAPTER II

THE winter passed. Famine was growing worse. Constant underfeeding and the impossibility of getting food created a curious sense of weakness and indifference. It was hard to say whether one had had dinner because we never had enough to eat. The dinner which we had to fetch from a 'communal kitchen' consisted of watery soup with millet in it and an occasional piece of rusty salted fish. It was so nauseating that had it been possible I would have stopped eating altogether.

In the spring the two senior forms in the commercial school where I taught were drafted into the Red Army. I was left almost without work, because I was no good at teaching small children. And in the autumn of 1919 it was proposed to reform all schools in a way which seemed to me entirely mistaken and which has not to this day led to any good or stable results. I loved teaching and was sorry to give it up after nine years of it.

For the summer we moved to Pavlovsk where there was a section of the Agronomical Institute that provided our baby with milk. My husband had to work for it during the long vacation, too.

Pavlovsk is a wonderful place. Petersburg is surrounded by marshy, neglected fields, poor kitchen-

17

gardens and patches of bright-yellow wild mustard; but here and there scattered like oases in the wilderness there are magnificent parks of the Imperial residences. It was one of the peculiarities of the old Russian life that in the times of serfdom the Tsars and the nobility created for themselves with the aid of foreign craftsmen places of fairy-like beauty that had nothing in common with the primitive surroundings in which the mass of the people lived. Thus, in Pavlovsk, a gifted English architect, Cameron, built a palace in the classical style.

The park looked fresh and lovely, and coming to Pavlovsk from the deserted capital, where we often recalled the sinister prophecy that 'Petersburg shall be left empty', we felt as though we had gone back a hundred years. It did not seem surprising to find in the glades instead of monuments to Marx and Lenin allegorical statues of Peace and Justice.

We had to live in the students' hostel in the so-called 'Constantine's Palace'. I must say, it was not much of a palace. The Emperor Paul I, who was always in a hurry, commanded that two palaces for the grand-dukes Alexander and Constantine should be built at Pavlovsk within something like a fortnight. A clever and resourceful architect, Brenna, brought some buildings from Tsarskoe, added a cupola, arranged a hall with a double row of windows, painted some winged griffons on the cornices and all was ready. Alexander's Palace has not been preserved, but Constantine's stands till now, looking like a tumble-down old barn.

Our room, like the rest of the palace, was almost in ruins: the marble fireplace had been taken out, loose bricks were showing; the wall-paper with pink

Chinese ladies and yellow pavilions was faded; the silk awning over the window was in tatters. There was no furniture except a deal table and a chair. We brought with us camp beds and a perambulator.

The students' dormitories were upstairs, and the ground floor halls were called 'laboratories': they were furnished with seats and tables roughly made of planks. In the big hall with double windows there was a piano taken from a house next door. The corner-room was converted into a kitchen. Twice a day three huge cauldrons were boiling in it: one with soup made of vegetables from the Institute's kitchen-garden – in the early summer it was chiefly sorrel and beetroot-tops; another with rye or wheat porridge, and a third with so-called coffee, i.e., drink made with baked oats. We ate and drank all this out of magnificent Sèvres china with the Imperial coat-of-arms and a design of a winding ribbon on which was written the motto 'Follow a straight path'. Little was left of this service by the autumn.

The Imperial china, the old palace that had seen better days, and the young crowd of students some of whom asked quite seriously, 'Comrade-professor, is a frog a unicellular or a multicellular organism?' some-how made the Revolution seem very real. The students worked in the fields, attended lectures, looked after the cows, and lived in the conviction that the future belonged to them. Sometimes it was very jolly to be with them, but often it was extremely unpleasant. For instance, after a long evening in the big hall when I had played the piano for them for hours, they would argue in the kitchen that there was no occasion to feed the professor's wife, for she was not really entitled to a ration. It was purely theoretical argument because there was enough food to go round; it showed, however, that some of them regarded us not as human beings like themselves, but as 'bourgeois' who may be utilised, but are not worth feeding.

But this did not worry me. In the long summer days, alone with my baby, I had other things to think about.

There had been a great change in him. His body was plump and firm, with delicious dimples all over, and he was strong and heavy. He showed great determination to get out of his pram, even if it were head downwards; he moved about vigorously, though chiefly on all-fours; he was keenly interested in everything that came his way – a stray leaf, a beetle, a blade of grass – and immediately stuffed it in his mouth. To extricate it was no easy matter and meant long and loud protests on his part. The few moments of peace I used to enjoy while he was having his bottle were no longer a rest, because now he needed careful watching: he tried to bite through the rubber teat if the milk did not come fast enough, or to throw the bottle out of the pram – and it would have been almost impossible to buy a new teat or bottle.

I fully grasped in those days what a blessing it would be to have a nurse, but that was out of the question, because we had no food to give her. With the greatest difficulty, at the price of my dinner and my daily ration of bread, I persuaded at last an old woman from the alms-house to come for a few hours a day, so that I might take on work at the Palace Museum.

This was the beginning of new work, which did not end till the day of my arrest.

To understand what it meant to work in a museum in U.S.S.R. it must be remembered that on the one hand, the museums were so rich in art treasures and so interesting that it was impossible not to be enthusiastic about the wealth of new material and new avenues of work opening before one at every step; on the other hand, the Soviet Government, though apparently anxious to preserve them, was really their chief enemy. It was ready at any moment to give away or sell everything they contained and to imprison or exile the curators for the least attempt to resist this. Needless to say, we were overwhelmed with work. Four or five of us in charge of the Palace Museum had to sort out the enormous quantity of art treasures that fell into our hands, to look after the upkeep of the place, to organise lectures and study-groups – and to do all this under appalling conditions, suffering from cold and hunger. Repairs had to be done but the simplest materials were lacking and workmen were hard to find.

I remember the first job I had to do. I was put in charge of the archives of the Pavlovsk Palace Museum.

'Mind you don't take alarm and desert us to-morrow,' the curator warned me, as he led me to the 'archives' section'.

Five big rooms were blocked up with bundles of old papers more than three feet deep.

'We had to bring these papers in a hurry from a building which the town has taken over. The Soviet officials were going to burn them. There are some more left, but those are in the old fortress tower which is not wanted, so they are comparatively safe there.'

In that tower the archives were piled up in huge heaps like snowdrifts in winter. The windows with broken panes were boarded up. Snow and rain could freely come in between the gaps in the boards.

If I had any instinct of self-preservation I should certainly have fled; but I remained. I carried the archives from the tower to the Palace, dried them, sorted them out, working in incredible dust, cold and damp. I could never have forgiven myself had I left all this to be simply destroyed. In a revolution everyone must bear full responsibility for his actions; everything has to rest on personal courage and initiative, until a new political organisation can take charge of the country. This was what I and all my fellow-workers believed.

For three years I toiled among the piles of papers and did not leave my job until all the records from 1777, the year when Pavlovsk was founded, to 1917, the year of the Revolution, were safely lodged in book-cases, numbered and sorted out in chronological order, ready for the future historian. It was only in Pavlovsk and in Gatchina that the whole of the palace archives were saved; in Tsarskoe Selo and Peterhof the Communist commissars used almost all of them for paper.

In sorting out the archives we discovered every day new names of artists, craftsmen, merchants, new data about the buildings, about planning the park, about the fêtes, the life of the times, the conditions of labour. A vivid picture of old Russia was rising before us.

Hungry and in rags, we fancied that we were doing great, important work in our Pavlovsk seclusion. Though it was only some twenty miles from Petersburg, the train journey took four to five hours, and during the three years I was there not a single Communist official looked in upon us except the specially

appointed commissar who under the old regime had
been in charge of the heating of the Palace. Not one of
the museum treasures was lost or damaged. We saw
that the art of the past attracted numbers of people
who had never heard of it before, and we felt that it
might really provide an impulse for building up a new
culture. Sometimes we actually fancied that the State
might be grateful to us some day. Alas! the three
of us who did most for Pavlovsk have all been
imprisoned since. It was the same thing elsewhere;
museum workers ended in prison or exile, and the art
treasures that they preserved so carefully during the
awful years of famine have been sold to foreign
countries.

·

CHAPTER III

THE winter, cold and dark, was terrible. We had to stay at Pavlovsk, living in one room, for it was easier to get firewood there. Life had become such a struggle for existence as perhaps even the cave-dwellers did not know; they were, at any rate, adapted to their surroundings, while we who had to do strenuous intellectual work felt completely helpless in the face of material difficulties.

A man in a torn overcoat tied round the waist with string to keep the warmth in, in boots made of an old carpet, with chapped hands and furtive, hungry eyes, was not a tramp but a professor or an academician. The women looked no better. The children were dreadful. I knew a baby of two, who had been taught by hunger not to finish his portion of bread at once, but to hide the crusts under the cupboard, among his toys or under the carpet. He wept if he could not find them again, but did not confide his secret to anyone until his little brother of four tracked him out and ate his supplies; then the baby angrily complained to the mother.

My baby had enough to eat because his father still received for his lectures a bottle of milk a day, but we were so starved that our health began to give way; I was developing heart trouble and my husband showed signs of tuberculosis.

24

Towards the spring we had come to the end of everything that could be sold or exchanged in the villages for potatoes, mangels or millet. Our salary was generally kept back two or three months and by the time it was paid we could not always buy with it a pound of butter, for the value of the rouble was falling rapidly. All were anxious to earn some extra money so as to escape death by starvation which was continually threatening everyone.

My only resource was literary work. Fortunately for the intellectuals a section of the Government was keen at that time on implanting a new and quite special sort of culture in the country – though, one would have thought, it was hardly the moment for it when a creeping paralysis was attacking railways, factories and electric power stations. Literature was to perform wonders: it had, in the shortest possible time, to re-educate the readers' tastes, to bring within their reach all the wealth of the world's cultural achievements, to expound the whole history of mankind from a new, Marxist, point of view and thus give the people 'a fresh weapon in the class struggle'. The Government devoted millions of paper money to these ends, but by the time that these sums had passed through various committees, editorial bureaux, censorship offices and so on, the authors' and translators' fees became a mere shadow. For translating a long novel of Balzac I received just enough paper money to buy two pounds of black bread; and my fee for writing a children's story in a magazine edited by Gorki amounted to the price of three lumps of sugar. Sometimes I felt so sick about the whole thing that I decided to give up literary work, but hunger soon weakened my resolution and

I looked out for a fresh job again. This time I thought I would try to get a commission from Grzhebin's, the only publishing concern that paid at once. It was rumoured that they did it in their own interests: on paying the authors and translators in advance, Grzhebin and Gorki obtained credits from the Government to cover the publishing expenses; it was said that with that money they bought paper in Finland and re-sold it at enormous profit to the news-papers which were in desperate straits for paper. Only a small proportion of the work they paid for was ever published.

Well, that was no concern of mine; all I wanted was to earn some money to keep us until May when my husband was going on a scientific expedition.

I was commissioned to re-tell, in a form interesting for modern children, Italian fairy tales for the series *Fairy Tales of all Nations* on condition that I did the work within a month. I had to read various collections of Venetian, Florentine, Neapolitan and Sicilian folk-lore, comparing the different versions. It was fascinating work and I enjoyed doing it, though I was weak with hunger and had to sit up till the small hours of the morning to finish the job in time. I felt shy about asking for my fee in advance, though we desperately needed the money. On the day that I went to Peters-burg to deliver the manuscript I very nearly fainted in the street, because I had not had anything to eat for the previous twenty-four hours and there was no food at home except a tea-cup of pearl barley for the baby. But the fee that I received on that memorable day was beyond my wildest dreams and I returned to Pavlovsk in triumph.

My husband, with the baby on his shoulder, met me at the station.

'I've brought heaps of money!' I said in answer to his look of interrogation. 'You'll never guess how much! 56,000 roubles! I am sure, no writer in a capitalistic country can boast of such a fee!'

'It only means thirty-five pounds of butter,' my husband said sadly. But of course he was delighted. That money simply saved us, and it was no use worrying about the real value of the rouble.

We sat up late that evening drinking oats 'coffee' with sugar, eating good black bread and butter and talking about the future. Life in the summer was always easier and perhaps things in general would get better. Surely, the Government would see that they could not go on like that.

My book was never published, and the manuscript was lost. Grzhebin was accused of something and his publishing business was closed. It was winter when I called at his former office. A disgruntled-looking intellectual, shivering with the cold, sat by a temporary iron stove sorting out manuscripts and using a good many of them as fuel.

'Your manuscript? How do I know what became of it?' she said bad-temperedly. 'There was no record kept. Everything is in a hopeless muddle. Some of the manuscripts are in Berlin, some are here, and there is absolutely nothing to go by. It's enough to drive one crazy. Haven't you got a copy?'

'No.'

'Well, then you must say good-bye to it. The devil himself couldn't find anything here.'

I was not surprised. It was the usual way in U.S.S.R.

Everything had always to be done in a desperate hurry, but almost before it was finished it proved to be of no use. Of nearly seven hundred pages that I wrote or translated only some eighty pages have been published, though all my work had been commissioned and paid for.

·

CHAPTER IV

A HAPPY TIME IN SPITE OF ALL

FAMINE lasted for about three years, from 1918 to 1921. For the Bolsheviks it was the period of 'military communism' when they felt ready to rebuild not only Russia but the whole world.

For the people it was 'famine' – no one calls that period by any other name.

The Bolsheviks, safely ensconced in their warm flats in the Kremlin, provided with special rations and guarded by the Tcheka and the Red Army, indulged meanwhile in the most daring and fantastic plans.

The people were dying off from typhus and famine. When villages and whole districts rose up in sheer despair, detachments of the Red Army exterminated the rebels – men, women and children – and burnt down the villages.

Strong-minded Communists merely shrugged their shoulders: if capitalists have a right to send millions to be slaughtered in senseless imperialistic wars, why not sacrifice a few scores of thousands for the sake of a happy socialistic future?

It was only when rebellion spread from villages to towns and there was a mutiny in the 'citadel of the revolution', Kronstadt, that Lenin made concessions and introduced *NEP* – the new economic policy – having first ruthlessly punished the mutinous sailors.

To the Communists NEP is a disgrace, a shameful retreat. The very reference to it is styled 'counter-revolution', even though Lenin himself introduced it 'in earnest and for a long time'.

For the country NEP meant deliverance from famine. The *prodrazvyorstka*, i.e., tax in kind imposed upon the peasants in an arbitrary way, utterly out of proportion to their means, was replaced by *prodnalog*, a tax which though still very high, was at any rate definitely fixed once for all. Trade on a small scale and small concerns of the home-industries type were allowed.

In the course of one year the country recovered to such an extent that bread, vegetables, butter, eggs, meat appeared on the market and ration cards somehow disappeared of themselves. There was enough food to go round.

Salaried workers and factory hands were worse off than the peasants at that time: pay was low and money did not recover its value at once, but anyway there was no starvation: if one could not afford meat, there was plenty of bread and potatoes – of which none but the Tchekists and Communists had enough during the famine.

It was said that the ideals of socialism grew somewhat dim during the period of NEP – but is it a crime against Socialism to have bread?

The intellectuals were, perhaps, in the worst position of all: we were paid very little, and the Communist supervision was not easy to bear. But the slackening of Government control and the recognition, in however small a measure, of private initiative, gave us more freedom in our work.

My personal affairs at that time took a bad turn: I
was dismissed from my post at the Pavlovsk Palace
Museum. After a few months, however, I was recalled
by the authorities and offered another job in the same
Commissariate. It appears that the Communist, who
was the cause of my dismissal, had himself fallen from
grace. To tell the truth, neither he nor I deserved such
a summary dismissal, but it is a peculiarity of the
Soviet Government that not being good judges of
character they do not trust anyone and build a great
deal upon accidental favouritism.

The Communist in charge of the museums was a
slow and stupid man.

'We've been a bit hasty about you,' he said without
the least compunction. 'We want you, so choose any
post you like.'

'Give me my old job at Pavlovsk,' I answered, for this
seemed the most sensible way of rectifying the 'mistake'.

'No, things are going well there, partly thanks to
you. Other portions of the museum front are quite
bare.'

He was not much of a talker and spoke in stereotyped phrases.

'I know every article in Pavlovsk and can answer for
my work,' I insisted.

The man picked up a calendar and not deigning to
reply to me wrote down 'Appointed to Peterhof from
May 15th.'

'On the fifteenth you must be at Peterhof.'

At that moment a dirty, dishevelled man looking
like a regular burglar, burst into the room.

'Comrade Timofeyev, here's an assistant for you: she

will take charge of the technical part, and you of management and administration. Don't make any trouble, and prepare a lodging for her.'

'I'm all right, it's all one to me,' the man answered gloomily.

That was the custom: non-party workers were put under the control of Communists, utterly ignorant, sometimes dishonest and invariably rude and suspicious. Our energies had to be divided between work and struggle against our overseers.

I knew that Peterhof included not one but ten palaces, beginning with the house of Peter I and ending with that of Nicholas II. They are scattered along the coastline some five miles long. Since the Revolution all the smaller objects in them had been taken for the sake of safety to the Big Palace and hastily deposited there without any arrangement. Some eight thousand objects had to be sorted out and returned to their original places; all the palaces were to be put into order in the course of the summer. There were not enough qualified assistants, and I had for helpers fourteen students of the Institute of Arts whom I had both to teach and to put on tasks which they were not competent to perform. That meant being on one's feet from nine o'clock in the morning till night. At the same time I was perfectly certain that as soon as I had done the chief part of the work the Communists would get rid of me because the post would then be a good one and somebody would want it. That was exactly what happened. But, still, it was a wonderful, and in its way, a happy time: I worked to my heart's content, and Peterhof, one of the most neglected show-places, became one of the best.

It was very exciting to come down early in the morning to the garden of Monplaisir – Peter the Great's summer residence. When I took charge of it they planted flowers there for the first time after the Revolution, put palms, laurel and orange trees in tubs and the 'fine kitchen-garden' came to life once more. The Tsar's house looked neat and clean as on a Dutch picture. An upholsterer was making curtains for the windows and the glass doors which till now had been whitewashed. A carpenter was restoring the oak panels to which the Dutch pictures were being returned from the Big Palace and the Hermitage. A cabinet-maker was repolishing the two-hundred years old Dutch furniture brought back from various offices where some of it had been taken in the days of Tsardom. The old members of the staff were happy to take up once more the work they loved. An old attendant, who had been at the Palace since Alexander II's reign, was so inspired by the work of restoration that he forgot all the wrongs he had had to suffer since the Revolution, after a lifetime of restful and honourable service.

He always met me with some piece of joyful news:

'Will you come and have a look at the kitchen?'

The kitchen decorated with Dutch tiles of the early eighteenth century had been washed spotlessly clean.

'I washed it myself, I climbed right up to the ceiling. I wouldn't let the charwomen do it, for fear they'd damage the tiles. I just let them do the floor because that's stone. Look at the pewter dishes in which oysters and pickled lemons used to be served to the Emperor Peter I – they are all here. But the faience ones have disappeared, though they are in the inventory.'

The old man put on his spectacles and sternly examined the inventory.

'Quite so. There should be eight large dishes and four small.'

'I have found some in the store-room,' I comforted him, 'and the Museum Fund will give us a few. I hope to bring them next week together with the missing pictures.'

'That's splendid! The public is very pleased. Working people particularly like our Palace. Last Sunday more than five hundred visitors came to see it.'

'And in the Big Palace there were over two thousand, they did not close till eight in the evening. They must have had fifty to sixty thousand during the summer.'

It was the same in all the ten palaces which were being turned into real museums, giving a clear picture of Russian life and culture for the last two hundred years.

The architect was having a struggle with the fountains, mending them, patching up the old pipes, thinking out new devices and, one after another, the fountains began to play.

'Just look at them!' the old workman in charge of them said delightedly, watching the strong jets of water fall into the basins.

Those old attendants were very helpful. Like us, they valued this remarkable place for what is of real worth in it. New attendants, as faithful and devoted, were being trained under them. And the general atmosphere of respect for the work and the art of the past had a sobering influence upon the unruly crowds that simply flooded Peterhof during the summer.

Weekdays and holidays I was at my work from

morning till late at night. I should not have had a
chance of being with my son at all had he not followed
me about everywhere riding on a stick, inventing all
sorts of harmless games for himself in the Palace halls
or playing by the hour in the sand by the beach
pavilions. He did not need a nurse now – every keeper
in the park was his bosom friend; all the dogs knew
him – he played with them and they came to the house
for food. He was growing up free, happy and trustful,
perfectly confident that the world – which did not
extend beyond Peterhof – was a lovely place.

During that time my gloomy overseer was looking
after the management, obviously not forgetting himself. Money desperately needed for repairs never
reached us. Everyone knew that he was a thief, and I
asked several times for an inquiry to be held. A committee was sent to see into the matter, but he gave
them such a fine meal and so much to drink that they
went back without doing anything. His doings did not
come to light till the autumn when he was put in
prison, in spite of his being a Communist – the sums
he had embezzled were enormous. And to think that
men like him, who had no scruples about stealing
public money, were put in charge of us, allowing us to
work as though it were a favour!

.

CHAPTER V

'BURN EVERYTHING'

'THE happy time' lasted about five years. In 1925 the Government failed to get from the peasants as much grain as they had reckoned upon. The peasants as a class have a strong sense of property; hard-working and obstinate, they felt themselves to be masters of the land they had obtained through the Revolution. The Government decided that they were an obstacle to the 'development of Socialism' and that the less amenable ought to be exterminated.

The struggle which the 'Socialistic' Government has been waging against the main bulk of the Russian population has assumed such proportions that the horrors of the Great War pale by comparison with the destruction wrought by the Soviet's agricultural policy.

The towns caught only the echoes of it, though these began to be pretty menacing as early as 1928. There was less food to be had, ration cards were re-introduced, prices began to soar, money decreased in value, the simplest objects such as paper, glass, nails, string, shoes, clothes, disappeared from the market.

'Another famine! If only death would come!' people said.

There were mass arrests once more, at first of the so-called 'speculators' and 'hoarders', i.e., of people who

36

were found to possess more than three roubles* in
silver or some jewellery, as though that were the
cause of the country's economic difficulties. Then came
the turn of the 'experts'. The Government was deter-
mined to put upon someone the blame for the famine
and general disorganisation which ushered in 'The
Five Years Plan'. It took us some time to grasp that we
were doomed, in spite of all the work we had done
utterly regardless of our own interests, and the fact that
there was no one to take our place. It was obvious that
the whole cultural life of the country would be under-
mined if qualified workers were exterminated, but
arrests and sentences of exile went on at a faster rate
than ever.

At that time I was assistant curator of the Hermitage
in the Section of Applied Arts. After several years of
practical and organising work I was given at last a
chance of devoting myself to study, but the order of the
Commissariate for Public Education dashed my hopes
to the ground. We were commanded in the shortest
possible time to reorganise the whole of the Hermitage
collection 'on the principle of sociological formations'.
No one knew what that meant; nevertheless, under the
guidance of semi-illiterate half-baked 'Marxists', who
could not tell faience from porcelain or Dutch masters
from the French or Spanish, we had to set to work and
pull to pieces a collection, which it had taken more
than a hundred years to create.

This was worse than the supervision of thievish
overseers who, at any rate, did not interfere with
museum treasures.

Hitherto, for all Russian intellectuals, life meant

* Six shillings.

work and work meant life. The more destructive the
Government policy was, the more strenuously we
worked to save what we could in our unhappy country.
Now things were getting beyond us. Blind terrorism
was the reward of thirteen years of labour under the
most trying conditions. OGPU reigned supreme everywhere, either openly or through party committees
interfering with all one did and striving to fit everything into the narrow and often senseless framework
of party instructions enforced by utterly ignorant
people. Everything had to be rearranged on 'Marxist'
lines. The way it was done can be judged from the
following conversation between the members of our
staff at the Hermitage.

'Do you know in what year feudalism came to an
end?'

'In what year? What are you talking about?'

'We've just been to a committee meeting for furthering Marxism and have been informed that feudalism
came to an end in 1495.'

'What nonsense is this?'

'Don't you see, it was the year of the discovery of
America!'

'Is it supposed to have been the same in all countries,
then?'

'The same everywhere. It was settled at the committee.'

'That's worth knowing!'

Another conversation, a month later.

'Have you heard the latest?'

'No, what?'

'Feudalism came to an end in 1848.'

'Another committee meeting?'

'Yes, and it's been settled for good. Keep it in mind.'

'And what about the discovery of America?'

'That's been cancelled. It's out of date, and to attach importance to it is "opportunism".'

'And how long will the decision of your committee be in force.'

'Till the next meeting, let us hope. Perhaps by then our Marxists will have read some other pamphlet.'

This was how young Communists implanted Marxism, while old and intelligent experts helplessly watched them do it. Everyone who protested was immediately declared to be a class-enemy and a 'wrecker'.

The Marxist authorities did not last longer than six months. They were replaced by others of the same stamp; the learned experts who happened to come into conflict with them were dismissed from their posts or found themselves in prison.

In that general atmosphere of strain and hopelessness I find it hard to remember what exactly happened in 1928 and in 1929. Everything was bad and growing worse until at last in 1930 there was such an outburst of mass terror aimed at 'the destruction of the intellectuals as a class' that all was forgotten and only one word – death – loomed before us.

For us personally the first warning was the delay of letters from Murmansk, where my husband was working at the time. Letters began to be seven or ten days late – the OGPU was reading them. It does not stand on ceremony or trouble to conceal its activities.

At the end of March I received a note from my husband that did not come through the post:

'S. and K. are arrested. My room was searched. I

cannot understand what they are after. Burn everything.'

Burn everything? Why, were we conspirators or
criminals? What does it mean – burn everything?
There is as much sense in burning tables and chairs as
in burning letters and photographs. The letters were
a record of friendship with people of high culture, the
only photographs I had were of those dear to me, my
family and friends of childhood and youth. Which of
them was I to burn? My father? I could not conceal
who he was even if I tried: he was one of the most
popular professors, an explorer of Siberia, a friend of
Nansen, the author of many scientific works whose
name could be found in every encyclopædia.* My
uncle? He, too, was a well-known professor, and many
generations of students have been brought up on his
textbooks. My sister? She was lecturer in two University schools. What could they find out about our life if
they examined every day and hour of it? Work –
almost since we were children. Hard work and service
to our country, without any personal advantage. And
here now we were 'suspects', as the aristocrats had
once been. It was too stupid and revolting!

Very well, I would burn everything I could, includ-
ing books with inscriptions from the authors, so as not
to compromise anyone by chance. If it had not been for
the boy who loved his home I think I would have
destroyed everything, so hateful was it to feel that
any day the OGPU agents would come and rummage
among my things, and look into all that was personal
and intimate.

Curse that Murmansk! I wished my husband had

* Professor V. Sapozhnikov.

not gone there. I have never seen a more gloomy and desolate place. The train journey of about a thousand miles takes more than two days and two nights. Wrecked railway carriages can always be seen lying beside the line – accidents are so frequent that there is not time to clear away the wreckage. At all the earth-works one sees groups of ragged and exhausted-looking exiles watched by an armed escort.

Murmansk is not a town but a bare, stony hollow in which are scattered some workmen's barracks, a few official buildings and the miserable wooden shanties of the local inhabitants. For eight months of the year the place is buried in snow-drifts, for two months in impassable mud and for another two in blinding dust. There are no fences, no causeways, no streets – or if there are, there is no understanding in what direction they are supposed to run, and it seems that privies and cesspools are in front of the houses and not behind them. At the bottom of the hollow one can see the ink-black water of the bay of Kola which never freezes in its rocky ice-bound banks. For more than two months in winter the town is plunged in polar darkness. There is not enough electricity, the lamps flicker and burn with a horrid reddish light that hurts one's eyes and makes one feel still more depressed.

And people consented to live in that cold, wretched hole because the first trawler industry in Russia was being organised there! I do think that devotion to one's work is a dangerous and incurable form of insanity. And what different kinds of people it attacks!

S. to whom my husband referred in his note was Shcherbakov. Solely owing to his exceptional intelligence he had risen from a 'boy' in a fishing business to be the manager of the northern section of a big fishing firm, and after the Revolution became one of the directors of the Northern Fisheries Trust. He had no family, no possessions; he lived as though the world held nothing but his beloved Fisheries Trust. One would have thought, the Government would value a man like that – but here he was the first to be arrested.

K. was Krotov, once an owner of big fisheries in the North. As soon as the Whites left Archangel, he gave to the Soviet Government all his property and set to work in the Fisheries as an ordinary employee. He, too, was in prison.

My husband's turn would evidently come next. He had indomitable energy and the mind of a true explorer; he always wanted more scope for his activities and was eager for new ventures. He might have quietly lectured at the University or at the Zoological Museum of the Academy of Science, but no – he would go to Murmansk to organise new scientific laboratories there! And now he would end in prison and exile, because the OGPU never spare a man who is above the average.

After those arrests my husband came to Petersburg in connection with his work and was able to live at home for a time. But he was so worn-out by the cross-examinations the OGPU had put him through that the words 'burn everything' seemed to overshadow the whole of our life and work. A reign of terror such as we had never seen before was drawing near. Not only we but all the intellectuals as a class were doomed.

CHAPTER VI

'48'

ON September 22nd, 1930, the *Pravda* came out
with the ominous headline 'The discovery of a
counter-revolutionary organisation to wreck the
workers' food supplies'. There followed column upon
column of incredible, overwhelming 'confessions'.
Specialists at the head of the main branches of food
supply, of the meat, fisheries and vegetable trusts –
well-known scientists and the best practical workers –
all were declared to be 'wreckers', confessed it and
signed their confessions. All the representatives of the
biggest concerns dealing with food-supplies were
included in the list, as though it were a case of elections
for some congress or conference.

My husband and I sat over the paper feeling utterly
overwhelmed. Rumours about arrests of specialists
had been accumulating all through the summer, but
most of the people had been seized during the last
few days. We had been afraid to think where this
was leading, but now the whole ghastly plan was
suddenly unfolded before us. All the best workers
were handed over to the OGPU – evidently, in order
to stop somebody's mouth and to involve hundreds of
others.

'But where are the facts?' I cried out at last. 'What
proof is there of their "wrecking"? No one has ever

43

heard of it! Why, many of the trusts mentioned here did remarkably well and actually made profits!'

I was choking with indignation at the cruelty and the shamelessness of it all, and at the same time I was horrified.

'Facts! It isn't a question of facts!' my husband said jerkily. 'They wouldn't scruple to invent them. Such absurd accusations . . . "criticising the rate at which the work was proceeding" . . . "having no faith in the Soviet Government's economic policy". These are crimes indeed! But that's not the point,' he concluded gloomily.

'What is it then?'

He passed me the paper and began nervously underlining with his nail separate words and phrases:

'Ryazantsev . . . "I have always been an enemy of the Soviet Government." Karatygin . . . "I have been drawn into the wreckers' organisation by Professor Ryazantsev." Levandovsky . . . "before I say anything about the wrecking" . . . Kuranov . . . "passing to my activities as a wrecker" . . . Drozdov . . . "I belonged to an organisation of wreckers" . . .'

'They go on like this, every one of them! They've all been made to say the same thing,' said my husband.

'But it's too silly and ridiculous! Who would believe that people could of their own will write or sign such confessions? And put it in such formal language, too.'

'The OGPU doesn't mind whether it is believed. The sentence will be the same for all, anyway – just as their confessions are the same.'

'Still, I can't understand how they could confess. Even under the threat of death. To make such confessions is as good as signing one's own death sentence,' I said, trying to shut out the obvious reflection that the whole point was the impudence with which the thing was stage-managed.

'One's own death doesn't matter, but what about one's family?'

'How do you mean? They are not after the families, surely? What use are we to them? And what can be more terrible for a family than to lose a father?'

My husband shrugged his shoulders.

'No,' I went on, trying to find comfort in words in which I was losing faith, 'it's impossible that they should shoot an old man like Ryazantsev, a professor, such an expert. . . .'

'But all those on the list are experts, all admirably qualified. The Communists themselves used to sing their praises and say they could not be replaced.'

'Surely they can't shoot them!' I persisted. 'Even if Ryazantsev gets ten years penal servitude, others will get five, and the rest may be simply sent into exile; after all, most of them were as good as in exile before – at Murmansk or on the Caspian – they can't send them much further, can they?'

'Yes, they can – to the next world.'

We were both silent. I saw the truth but I did not want to see it. It was clear from the choice of names that they had all been marked down as victims, that the defiant and pitiless tone of the newspaper was not an accident, and yet I could not reconcile myself to the obvious. One may very well know that terrorism is part of political tactics, but it is unthinkable to take it for granted.

'But why? What sense is there in destroying people who worked, invented new methods, created new branches of Soviet industry?' I asked helplessly.

'Why? To begin with because the Five Year Plan cannot be carried out and they have to justify themselves somehow in the eyes of the workmen and the foreigners, and secondly, the OGPU has been hard hit by the timber works being closed; they can't get credits if they don't frighten the Government. Or perhaps they simply want unpaid labour – I can't tell, I know nothing about politics.'

'But why should they shoot them?'

'I don't know. We do not know how many have been arrested besides those whom they forced to sign the confessions – or whose signatures they forged. It is obviously only the beginning.'

At work everyone was excitedly arguing about the same thing, trying to keep out of earshot of the Communists and spies: everyone was conscious of the approaching catastrophe and tried to find comfort in arguing that reason and justice were on our side.

After office hours in all Government institutions, factories and even schools, compulsory meetings were held at which 'unanimous' resolutions demanding death sentence for the accused had to be passed. After the meetings the people were made to march in rows along the streets carrying placards hastily made of red cotton bearing inscriptions in black:

'The verdict of the working class is unalterable – the wreckers must be wiped off the face of the earth.'

'Death to the wreckers!'

'Death to the counter-revolutionaries!'

'Death to all the enemies of the Soviets!'

At those meetings wives, sisters, fathers, brothers, even children, had to vote for the immediate death-sentence on their near and dear ones who had been arrested in hundreds during the preceding few days. Those who ventured not to hold up their hands in favour of the death-sentence were immediately summoned to the 'local committee', cross-examined and told that they would have to leave their posts.

'Remember, those who are not with us, are against us,' was the concluding remark of the examining officer.

Several workmen and simple-hearted Communists asked whether there would be a legal trial for the accused, and wondered why 'the wreckers' had been tolerated for so many years. They were at once summoned to the 'party committee', then sent to prison and afterwards into exile. All the others kept a frightened silence as though they had themselves been sentenced to death and with pale, resigned faces marched behind the blood-red placards.

There were two more days of ominous newspaper hysteria, ferocious speeches at the meetings 'to stir up public opinion', and OGPU motors hooting day and night as they rushed about the streets collecting their victims and terrorising the population. On September 25th the awful list was published:

(1) A. V. Ryazantsev, professor, gentleman by birth, member of the board of directors of the Central Cold Storage Trust . . . founder of the counter-revolutionary organisation

(2) E. S. Karatygin, professor, chairman of the Agricultural Section . . . leader of the counter-revolutionary organisation

(3) M. Z. Karpenko, gentleman by birth, head engineer of the Cold Storage Centre ... organiser of wrecking activities at the Cold Storage Centre

(4) S. P. Nikitin, deputy-chairman of the Volga-Caspian Fisheries Trust . . . leader of counter-revolutionary activities there

(5) P. I. Karpov, technical director of the Net and Tackle Trust . . . organiser of wrecking the work of the Trust

(6) Shcherbakov, managing director of the Northern Fisheries Trust . . .

and so on, forty-eight names – forty-eight men full of life, men of exceptional knowledge and experience – and one short phrase 'to be shot'.

There was still a tiny, faint hope that the death-sentence had been commuted to penal servitude – but no!

'The sentence has been carried out,

'Chairman of the OGPU Menzhinsky'.

We felt exactly as though the OGPU agents had suddenly walked into the various offices and shot those who were in charge of the work. There were no blood-stained bodies on the floor, but essentially it was just the same. The empty desks of the murdered men stood in the usual place; their papers had for the most part not even been disturbed by the OGPU who had 'documents' of their own to incriminate them. Those who had not been arrested as yet wandered about the

office in utter bewilderment. All felt that death was
near and there was no escape.

In prisons the shootings continued on the quiet but
OGPU published no more lists of victims. It was said
that the death sentences had made a bad impression
abroad. Arrests went on at such a rate that in some
departments of the main Government institutions
there were only typists and caretakers left.

. . . .

Two days after the shooting of the 'forty-eight' a
little girl, the stepdaughter of one of the victims, ran to
us in alarm.

'Mother has sent me. Yesterday they came and made
a list of all our things and to-day they've come to take
them away. They've taken all we have, everything . . .'
her lips trembled, her eyes were full of tears, but she
was in a hurry to give her mother's message. 'Mother
has just received a notice, they are sending her into
exile, she has to go somewhere very far, and she asked
perhaps I could live with you for a time. Mother thinks
perhaps they won't exile me because daddy was not
my real, I mean, not my own father.' She corrected
herself and suddenly burst into tears. 'But I loved him
very much, and I do love him still, and the girls in our
class voted that daddy should be shot. I won't, I won't
go to school any more,' she cried through her sobs.

'There, there, pull yourself together. Where is your
mother now?'

'She's gone to . . .' the child's eyes opened wide with
terror, 'mother said she was going to the OGPU.
They'll shoot her there as they shot daddy!' she sobbed.

'Nonsense, they won't touch her. Why, you saw that
she went there herself, she wasn't taken like daddy. I

expect she wants to ask them if she may leave you behind.'

'I don't want to be left, I want to go with mother.'

The child wept so bitterly, hiding her face in my lap, that my hands and dress were wet with her tears.

'Of course you will be with mother, only you will go to her later, when she is settled. Listen: mother will get there, find a room, find some work, then write to us here and you will go to her. Just think, other people are worse off than you: there's one mother who has two small children, and she isn't allowed to leave them here – and in the place to which they are sending her there are no hotels, and she doesn't know a soul there and will have nowhere to go from the station. It will be much nicer for your mother to travel by herself, and I will soon send you to her. And you need not go to school here.' I was trying to comfort the poor child with the misfortunes of others.

'You know, they are sending into exile that mad woman, too.'

'Surely not?'

'Mother said so. Her sister will go with her; she can't travel alone.'

'Well, you stay here and I'll go and see your mother,' I said, freeing myself from the child's grasp as I saw that she was getting calmer. I could not imagine what her mother's state must have been.

It was too outrageous. Women, stunned with grief, and frightened children who could not grasp what had happened and watched, horrified, their mothers' despair, were being sent into exile, robbed of all they possessed except a change of clothes. Within three days of the fathers' execution the families had to leave for

remote little towns, with no money, no help of any
kind, not knowing where to put up, for it was extremely difficult to find living room anywhere. Perhaps it was the very depth of their despair that saved
these unhappy women. They signed notifications of
exile and protocols of confiscation, hardly grasping
what it all meant, and, taking their children, set off in
utter hopelessness into the unknown. Their fate created
perhaps even more panic than their husbands' death,
and apparently this was precisely what the Government wanted for their campaign of terror.

In the meantime, people who were not directly
threatened with anything, broke down in the general
atmosphere of strain and fear, and committed suicide.
Learned experts, some of the honest Communists,
museum and scientific workers, for the most part
comparatively young people, hastened to take their
own lives. The numbers of suicides increased so rapidly
that the papers were forbidden to mention them.
Elderly people died a natural death, but a sudden one:
their hearts nurtured on Liberalism and Tolstoy could
not stand this new 'Communist offensive'.

No more than a week had passed after the execution
of the 'forty-eight', but one might have thought that the
intellectuals had been stricken by plague: thousands
were in prison, and those that were still free were a
pitiful sight. No one argued any more or talked of
justice or felt secure in the sense of his own rectitude.
Prison, death or exile were the fate of all; it would
have been shameful to expect mercy, when one's
friends lay buried in a nameless grave, and their
widows and children suffered in far-off exile.

·

CHAPTER VII

LAST DAYS

ONLY Soviet citizens know what it means to wait for arrest, prison, and almost certain death when one has not done any wrong.

After the shooting of the 'forty-eight' we went about as though we had been poisoned, looking round at every step, starting at every sudden noise, alarmed by everything. The day dragged on wearily. There seemed to be no strength left for work, though sometimes one did it with a kind of desperate energy, to try and forget one's thoughts. Four o'clock brought a certain sense of relief: we had not been arrested at the office, that meant we would be able to go home once more. And at home one felt more wretched than ever: the rooms and the furniture seemed hostile in their cold sameness and indifference.

My husband and my son came home, and it seemed as though this were our last evening, our last meal together; I could hardly swallow any food, thinking either of the friends who had perished so suddenly, or wondering how much longer my husband would still be with us.

The boy was watching us with frightened eyes. He knew that friends who had such a short time before been well and cheerful, had been to see us, had joked with him, were now killed — but he could not understand why and how. The little girl who sadly sat beside him was a living reminder of their dreadful and incomprehensible fate.

He felt nervous when it was time to go to bed.

'Will you sit beside me?' he asked pitifully.

'Yes, of course. You get into bed.'

He hid under the bedclothes; we talked of various things, then were silent, trying to hide our thoughts from each other. The child seemed more grown-up every day.

'Mother, why were people so cruel in the old days?'

'How do you mean?'

'They persecuted Galileo and Copernicus.'

I explained to him how far the story he had heard at school of Copernicus and Galileo was true. He had been told that both men were simply fighting against religion and the Church and – for the sake of simplifying matters – that both were burnt at the stake by the Inquisition.

'And now?'

'Now?' I repeated, though I knew perfectly well what he meant.

'Why do they shoot people now?'

Poor, poor boy, whose childish mind had to ponder such problems!

'Go to sleep, darling, it's late. I'll tell you another time.' Obediently and wearily he closed his eyes, guessing that I had no answer to give him.

I understood what his question meant: he thought that if he knew why people were put to death, he might find out whether his father would be shot. His father was still at home, but we dared not believe in his safety. We were glad of every day that passed hoping that time might save him.

'Mother, how many Decembrists did they shoot in 1825?'

'Five?'

'And when Lenin's brother tried to kill the Tsar?'

'Also five. Only they were hanged and not shot.'

'Does that make any difference?'

I said nothing, because I had not the strength to speak.

'Mother, and why was it so many this time – forty-eight?'

'Times are different. You'll understand some day; it's not so simple.'

Not so simple! As though human life had grown cheaper and killing meant something different!

When the boy dropped asleep, time dragged on more slowly than ever. My husband and I had nothing to hide from each other: we sat on the sofa and waited. What were we waiting for? There is only one thing that everyone waits for at night, when every minute is filled with the strain of expectation – the OGPU.

Ten o'clock. It was too early for them. We were talking of something else, but more and more slowly and absent-mindedly.

Eleven o'clock. They might come soon now. Loud steps were heard in the yard . . . on the stairs. . . . My heart throbbed desperately. No, it was not here.

Twelve o'clock. They might come any minute.

'That was how they took F.,' my husband recalled. 'He had just come home from the office – he had some work to finish and stayed there till midnight. What

donkeys we are! How we have worked – and all to
earn a bullet through the head!'

'Poor, dear F.! How kind he was, and naíve as a
child! He trusted everyone.'

We could scarcely hold back our tears. It seemed
unthinkable that that man whom everyone had loved
for his sweet disposition, who had never hurt anyone,
had been disgraced as a 'wrecker' and killed.

Time crept on more and more slowly. Every minute
seemed to drag. There were footsteps in the yard:
people were returning from evening work, from the
theatre. . . . Some came up our stairs, others walked
past, but I listened breathlessly to them all. My mouth
was parched; I felt cold and then hot all over. There
was a pain at my heart as though it had been bruised.

One o'clock in the morning. The yard was growing
quiet; the gates were locked. Half an hour passed
quietly. Suddenly there was a sharp ring at the gate.
There they were . . . sure to be. Thud of footsteps
and loud conversation. No, two drunken men.

Two in the morning. The trams stopped. Everything
seemed still. . . . No! There was the hoot of a motor
car . . . the OGPU car. The revolting, piercing sound
came nearer and nearer. . . . No, it went past.

Every time my heart throbbed, ready to burst; I
listened, trembling. When danger was over, I felt
limp and cold and weak. Was it because we were
cowards? No, it was not death we feared; it was unbearable to feel oneself at the mercy of a stupid, cruel
tyranny from which there was no defence, no escape.

Three in the morning. It was late, but they still
might come. The OGPU had so much 'work' just now
that they were at it all night. And so we sat up till

daybreak. If one dropped asleep, dreams were worse than reality. In sleep one loses one's will-power and suffers more acutely and hopelessly.

'People are afraid of wild beasts, of bears,' said my husband, following his strange, weary thoughts. 'But a bear doesn't attack one, if he has had enough to eat. And one doesn't go empty-handed to fight a bear. But *they* will goad me like a beast in a cage. Oh, if only the end would come soon!' he cried out suddenly.

'Hush, you will wake the boy.'

That was how we, women, tried to slur things over: telling the boy 'go to sleep, it's late' and the father, 'don't wake the boy'.

We had a month of it, night after night. Sometimes, in utter exhaustion my husband said:

'Let me die. It will make things simpler: they won't touch you and the boy if I am gone.'

'You mustn't talk like that. Let us think of something else.' We took an atlas and looked at maps. A free, wide world was unfolded before us, calling us away. There people might be poor, might be suffering from the economic crisis, but anyway they were free. In the map of U.S.S.R., from Yakutsk to Karelia all the swamps, tundras and wild forests were centres for penal camps. Their population numbered over a million although the mortality in them was more than sixty per cent a year.

'If they send us to the Far East, we might try to escape just here,' said he, pointing to the map. 'And then to Japan — they won't give us away there.'

'Not much chance of being sent there, and from Yakutsk it is far to the frontier. I only hope it won't be to Solovki.'

'You are wrong there. The only danger in Karelia is the swamps.'

We long gazed at the map trying to think of future ways of escape.

'The Caspian is the worst of all,' my husband said. 'They are making penal camps there, too.'

'Why is it the worst?'

'Sea, sandy desert, and they say that Turks give away the escaped prisoners. But still it may be possible even there. We'll escape, won't we?'

'We will,' I answered firmly.

CHAPTER VIII

THE END OF FAMILY LIFE

A CATASTROPHE always comes suddenly, however long one may have been expecting it. We had endured a month of agony at nights, listening to every sound, and it happened almost in the daytime, as we came home from our work. It is easy not to find people at home at that hour, but an obliging Communist colleague rang up my husband upon the telephone.

'Are you at home? How are you?'

'Do you want anything of me?'

'No, nothing. I just wanted to ask if you were going away.' A quarter of an hour later the OGPU agents came with an order for my husband's arrest.

I was kept late at the office and when I came home all was over. Hardly anything had been touched: the search had been quite perfunctory, because the OGPU did not really care to find out the true state of things. A young man in civilian clothes lolled in an armchair, smoking a cigarette.

That was all. But our *home* was gone. Life seemed to have gone out of everything around us. We moved about: my husband changed his clothes, packed his suit-case. I helped him in silence, but we did it quite mechanically. It all seemed unreal.

When all the formalities and preparations were over

we sat down to tea, but we did not drink it. One could not swallow a single mouthful.

We had to wait for the OGPU car: with the great number of arrests, there were not enough cars to go round. We sat in silence, looking at each other for the last time. How many men had left home like this and never come back!

An hour passed. The OGPU young man made himself quite at home: he rang up his friends on our telephone, examined books and pictures, walked about the room, carelessly opened and shut the drawers -- he was master here. We sat stiffly without moving and looked at each other in silence. One could not speak in front of an OGPU agent. And indeed, what could one say during those last moments?

What happiness it is, I thought, to be still able to look at him, to see his tired face, pale and set. I knew that he was afraid of making the least movement for fear of losing his self-control, and I felt just the same. I gazed at him fixedly trying to imprint every feature in my memory for ever: his head was slightly bent with an expression of utter weariness, his hair had begun to turn grey, the corners of his mouth were twitching slightly, his eyes . . . but one can't look into a man's eyes at such moments.

'How much longer will you be? Hurry up!' the OGPU young man said over the telephone.

We started. The boy had not come home yet. Will the father have to go away without saying good-bye?

What a good thing I had sent the little girl to her mother! But there evidently was still time. We sat looking at each other as before. He, too, was probably trying to fix my face in his memory. I had grown an old woman during those days. For two hours we were sitting thus, saying good-bye as before death. Every minute that passed, one's heart grew heavier with the impending sense of loss. And our son was not at home. Poor child, what awaited him!

At last there was a ring.

'It's our son,' I said. 'May I open the door?'

The OGPU agent nodded.

I let in the boy, and before I had had time to say anything he rushed forward in alarm and stood stock-still seeing a stranger by his father's side. He sat down, poor child, and looked at us silently, not understanding what it all meant, what we were waiting for and why we looked at each other so strangely. He was trembling all over, not daring to ask anything.

The OGPU car hooted outside.

'Come along.'

We all stood up. This was the end.

For the last time we saw him come up to us to say good-bye, doing his utmost to control his emotion. We could not utter a single word. He held out his hand to me and the boy, looked at us for the last time, and walked out of the room. We let him go his sorrowful way and looked after him in silence.

.

CHAPTER IX

ALONE

THAT night there was nothing to wait for, no need to listen to anything. I put the child to bed and sat down beside him. His father was in prison; we were alone in the world. To-morrow everyone would shun us like the plague. No help could come to us from anywhere. All that was left me in life was that corner by the child's bed, in the light circle of the lamp beside it, and somewhere, in incredible distance, the OGPU prison, his father and . . . perhaps, death.

The boy could not go to sleep; as soon as he dozed off he woke again with a pitiful cry, looked at me with frightened eyes, touched me with his little hands to make sure that I was still there and had not disappeared into the unknown like his father.

I sat without any thoughts, as during those two hours when my husband and I were looking at each other. His pale, weary face was before me – that was all.

Tired out, my son dropped asleep at last, his face looking sad and thin. I had to go and clear up the study after the search. I went to the door and stopped . . . It was so difficult to go into the room that would never see him again.

I opened the door. The room smelt of the cigarettes that the OGPU agent had been smoking.

Never, never again could I get rid of the visible or invisible presence of the OGPU! I did not know how long it would be before I, too, would be arrested – it was usual to imprison whole families. All Soviet citizens were in a noose which the OGPU tightened as they thought fit.

Burning anger filled my heart when I sat down to the writing-table, littered with papers, books and photographs, chucked on to it by the OGPU agent.

What did they care about ideas, about culture! They only needed it for newspapers and magazines published for the benefit of credulous foreigners. There they wrote about the bright new life being created in the U.S.S.R., about the wonderful progress of science upon which Socialism was being built. And here? How many of our professors and academicians had been spared? And those who were not imprisoned yet, in what conditions had they to work?

I got up to return to my room, but in the dark stumbled against the bed. The shirt which my husband had taken off before going lay on it. Not thinking what I was doing, I took it, pressed it to my face, and burst into sobs. Despair mastered me at last.

I do not know how long I lay there crying – the shirt was wet with my tears. Suddenly a far-off image dating back to my childhood rose in my weary brain.

Chloe in *Uncle Tom's Cabin*. Tom is sold and Chloe is sobbing over his shirt, pressing it to her broad, black face. As a child I wept over poor Tom, as millions of other readers had wept before me, and now I was myself like Chloe. We had become slaves in 'the freest country in the world'. Tom was sold, and all I could hope for was that my husband should be 'sold' too and not shot. Perhaps, since he was a highly-qualified expert, the OGPU would sell him to some other institution so as to receive 90 per cent of his earnings; then he would live. He would live like a slave. Without a home, without freedom or initiative, he would work while there was any strength left in him — and that would be a blessing, if, indeed, life was a blessing at all.

.

CHAPTER X

EMPTY DAYS

I DO not know how to describe the days of blank misery that followed my husband's arrest. Arrest in those days was almost equivalent to a death sentence. Every day might also be my last day of freedom. It seemed so much simpler to die – but I had to live because two other lives depended on me: a man's life there, in prison, and the life of the child who watched with helpless wonder the disappearance of the dear familiar faces around him.

The newspapers were full of events as in the days of war. First there was the horrible 'Industrial Party' trial, when Ramzin, casually remarking that 'about 2,000 people were connected with his organisation' openly declared at the cost of how many lives he had bought his own. Then there were preparations for the 'academic trial', which dealt a death-blow to Russian science, especially to historical research; the fate of the accused was settled by the OGPU behind the scenes, for they obviously lacked the dramatic talent of Ramzin and Co. Finally, there was the disgraceful 'Trial of the Mensheviks', when former members of the Communist party made confessions and obsequious apologies, giving each other away. All this increased the sense of utter devastation that had come over the Russian intellectuals.

64

The more sentences of death and of penal servitude were passed, the more indifferent everyone became. It was no longer a case of individual people perishing, a whole class was being wiped out. It was like an avalanche or a hurricane sweeping everything on its way.

Soon we were going to have a general 'sifting', i.e., an overhauling of the personnel of various institutions; the OGPU had not time as yet to take up each case individually.

The sifting was announced by huge placards posted both inside and outside the buildings. They were all after the style of the one that said, 'Comrade, denounce your comrades, priests, bourgeois, and other counter-revolutionaries'. The wording was somewhat unfortunate, but essentially correct. Under the placards stood a huge letter-box in which the denunciations were to be dropped.

Then, since according to Marx, everything must be based upon 'the principle of productive relations', learned and scientific institutions were attached to big factories, and factory hands were put on committees to investigate the 'trend' of the work and the suitability of the staff.

Good old workmen who had been minding machines for the last twenty years, and uppish young men of the new type – machinists, electricians, stokers, were brought into laboratories and studies filled with books. They were shy, astonished, interested, and utterly at a loss what to believe. It all seemed to them rather like black magic. It was hard to decide whether all these books and those elderly, spectacled scholars were doing good or harm to the proletarian state.

It looked as though the sifting might prove a failure, and 'the class enemies' would not be detected. Then members of the OGPU and the Communist party confined the inquiry to the social origin of the intellectuals, their liking for the old regime and so on. So-and-so had once held a post in such-and-such a ministry, so perhaps he was a friend of the Minister. That man's wife was a countess or a princess by birth, or a general's daughter, or something of the sort. This one, though he was not a gentleman by birth, like the others, continued to write in the old spelling; and that man there said 'gentlemen' instead of 'citizens' or 'comrades'.

Such a method greatly simplified matters, and soon most of the experts and specialists received notices of dismissal 'in the 1st category' – i.e., without the right to seek employment elsewhere. They looked back in surprise at their fifteen or twenty years of good, useful work, unable to understand what wrong they had done. They did not know which way to turn. All their life had been bound up with the institution from which they were so arbitrarily driven away. The younger men were wondering what kind of work they could adopt instead of their speciality.

The sifting lasted for a couple of months. When it was over, the authorities, after bidding amiable good-bye to the bamboozled workmen, began to understand that the work of the learned institutions could not be carried on. There was no one to replace the highly-qualified specialists who had been dismissed, and so most of them were 'temporarily' left at their posts. But time had been lost, work interrupted, people's nerves racked – all for the sake of a show of 'proletarian watchfulness'. The departments of art and science which so far had been comparatively safe, were gradually being destroyed also: the OGPU was doing away with the more gifted and prominent people, the Party and Local Committees were breaking up the institutions by their 'siftings'. We watched in misery the devastation all around us, and many whispered in despair that there must be some real 'wreckers' in the OGPU or in the Political Bureau, bent on making all cultural work impossible and destroying the intellectuals in order that ... though no one could surmise what could possibly be the object of it.

But I did not care any longer. All I could think of was that my husband was in prison, that I too might be arrested any moment and our boy would be left utterly alone. It seemed to me at times simply stupid to try and carry on the work which I no longer cared for now that it was deprived of all meaning. It was a desperate struggle to keep it up; winter, cold, hunger were upon us, and it was almost more than one could bear, especially when to one's ordinary duties was added the request to take part in 'social work'.

Four o'clock, the end of the working day, but there was a general meeting to attend. One way out of the Hermitage was closed and the other was guarded by Communists from the local Committee.

'Four o'clock – the boy has come home from school. The rooms are cold. The stove hasn't been heated. Would he bring in some logs? He does not like going down to the shed, and really they are too heavy for him to carry.'

The meeting had not begun yet: the Communists in

command were late. Everyone was tired and hungry. The hall was cold. Some walked about, wrapped up in their overcoats, others sat huddled up. Everyone felt wretched, but could not go away.

At last the 'chiefs' appeared.

'The work of building up a Socialistic state proceeds by laying the foundations' . . . the official orator rattled off the hackneyed phrases to which no one listened.

'The child is sure to be famished' came into my mind. 'It will soon be five o'clock. I wonder if we have any oil for the primus? He wouldn't think of calling at the shop, and everything will be closed at six.'

' . . . calls for energetic action, for an effort of our proletarian will . . .'

'He is sure to buy the bread. I left the ration-cards* on the table. I hope he won't eat the whole loaf, or there will be nothing left for the morning.'

' . . . with gigantic strides. Industrialisation of the whole country . . .'

'I simply must get away before six, or I'll be too late for the Co-op. There's nothing at home except yesterday's potato soup.'

' . . . Boldly overtaking capitalistic Europe decaying under the pressure of the economic crisis . . .'

'No, I can't stand this any longer. It will soon be six, there will be no time to do his home lessons.'

My anxious thoughts kept time with the empty words. We were all bored to death, and he was shouting the same thing for the hundredth time. Everyone was longing to go home but was afraid of being

* The ration was ½lb. white and ¼lb. brown bread a day per person.

noticed and called to task. At last I could not endure any more. I slipped out and rushed downstairs as though I were chased. In the hall I ran against a young Communist who was on guard there, but I put on my overcoat defiantly before his very eyes.

'Where are you off to, comrade? Surely the meeting isn't over yet?' came the malicious question.

'No, but I have to go to my evening work.'

'Oh, is that so?' he drawled spitefully, not believing me. 'Don't forget that there's a sifting going on.'

I was not listening. I was caught, anyway. It was no use going back. And I wouldn't do it, I was not going to let the child go hungry till night time.

The frost was getting sharper. It was 18-20 R. I walked as fast as I could to be in time for the Co-op.

Empty counters. On the shelves there were packets of mustard and bay leaf. I looked about desperately to see if there was anything eatable – no, nothing! There was a barrel of salted herrings, but one could only buy them on ration-cards, from $\frac{1}{2}$ lb. to 1 lb. per month. There was a barrel of green salted tomatoes, but they looked so flabby and horrid that one could only buy them from sheer despair.

The shop assistant was wearing his fur coat because the place was hardly ever heated. Blue with cold, bored and cross, he muttered morosely:

'What do you want? I haven't got anything.'

At that moment I saw a jar of artificial honey in the corner of an empty shelf.

'Honey, please.'

Reluctantly he took it off the shelf and pushed it into my hand in silence, without wrapping it up. I paid 2 roubles 80 copecks for ½lb. of yellow sweetish syrup. Anyway, it would be a treat for the child.

Here was my door. I rang the bell. I heard him running to the door. What a joy it was that I could still hear his footsteps, that I was just going to see his dear little face. But his father? . . . Would he ever see the child again?

'Why, mother, it's six o'clock! Just look – six! I am hungry.'

'Have you bought any oil?'

'No. The queue is several streets long. I should freeze to death if I stood there, hungry. There is a little left in the can.'

'Have you brought up any logs?'

'No. It's so dark in the shed.'

'What a boy you are! We'll perish of cold at that rate.'

'And why were you so late?'

'Late! There was a general meeting, and you know there's a sifting going on. I've been caught as it is.'

'You can't even run away properly!' he said, laughing, glad to be no longer alone. His little face looked pinched with hunger. It was cold in the rooms and still colder in the kitchen; we did not heat it – fuel was scarce, and we had nothing to cook. We used a primus.

'Well, shall we go down for the logs now?'

'Mother!' he said piteously, 'mother, I am hungry! I have had nothing since midday at school, and it was precious little too – just millet porridge and no milk or sugar with it, only dirty-looking gravy.'

I gave in, because I too had had nothing since breakfast, and running about in the frost made me giddy with hunger. We went into the kitchen to warm up the soup.

'What else is there?'

'Nothing, darling. I haven't had time to go to the market. I've bought some honey at the Co-op.'

'Well, never mind, we can have some tea. I brought a loaf, and, you know, it's not very stale. . . . I've only eaten a little piece,' he added, catching my look of alarm.

We never had new bread because by the time it was brought from the central bakeries to the depots and distributed among the district bakeries it was a day or two old. There is no need to say that no pure wheaten bread was baked; it always looked greyish.

The boy saw to the primus, chattering all the time like a bird released from a cage, and I cut up potatoes for our second course.

'Well, so they haven't turned you off yet?'

'Not yet.'

'What shall we live on, if they do?'

'I'll get some other job. If only they don't lock me up!' The words escaped me. I had no one to talk to. I was afraid of compromising my friends, and indeed I felt far off from everyone, but the boy shared my sorrow and trouble.

'And what shall I do all by myself, mother?' he asked piteously, and tears came into his eyes.

'Go to school. Wait for me. Take food to daddy and me in prison – you know there's no one else to do it. Why, look, the Ivanovs are both in prison, father and mother, and there are five children left. Only the little girl is older than you, but they manage somehow. . . . Better come and have supper.'

It is dreadful to think of the number of children left to themselves. A few days ago a young woman who died of consumption was being buried. Her husband was in the Shpalerny prison. A few days before her death he had been sentenced to penal servitude at Solovki. He was not allowed to go and say good-bye to her, and she was too weak to get up. Only two children, a boy and a girl, stood by her grave, holding hands, like the children in some heart-rending fairy-tale.

Just as we sat down to supper there was a ring at the bell. What new trouble was this? After my husband's arrest no one came to see us.

'From the house-committee,' declared a nasty-looking, one-eyed old man, former porter at the house next door and now a Communist.

'What is it?'

'Have you two rooms?'

'Yes.'

'You'll have to move into one. It's too much for you. What do you want with two rooms?'

'I have a right to them; mother and son are not supposed to share a room.'

'Right, indeed! Much I care about rights when there isn't room for people! Would you have me put working men in the basement and leave you gentry nice and comfortable?' he shouted in a horrid, high-pitched falsetto.

'I tell you I have a right to the room, and I will stick up for it.'

'We shall see!' he said menacingly. 'You'd better remember where your husband is!'

He went away, swearing at me at the top of his

voice as he walked downstairs. The boy clung to me in alarm.

'What will he do to us, mother?'

'Nothing, don't you mind him. He is just trying to frighten us, but he can't do anything.'

Alas, I knew that he could do a great deal, and not merely by his rudeness and impudence. He guessed that I might be arrested any day and hastened the hour by sending in reports to the OGPU, anxious to let the rooms – the most precious thing in U.S.S.R.; he could easily get a bribe of two or three thousand roubles for them and sell the lease for five or six thousand.

Our soup had gone cold. We no longer felt hungry. Attacks of the house-committee is the worst thing, next to OGPU, because they threaten to rob one of one's home – the last refuge in that dreadful life.

Then there was another trouble.

'Mother, you know, the bath is frozen,' sadly said my little boy as though it were his fault.

'When? I had a bath this morning.'

'When I came back from school. The water doesn't run.'

'Just our luck! Well, put on your coat, let us go and get the logs.'

'What about my prep?' he asked timidly.

'There'll be time for that. Hurry up! We don't want to be frozen out.'

We went to the shed. The door was frozen so fast that we could hardly push it open. The heavy logs were covered with ice. Bruising our hands we could scarcely manage to drag them up the stairs.

'Daddy would have heated the stove for us!' said the boy.

'Yes, daddy. . . . It's a good thing he doesn't know our troubles.'

At last we lit the stove in the room and in the bathroom; the water might melt after all. We sat by the fire boiling a kettle on the embers and doing home lessons. He had to learn a poem.

> Machines and sinews
> Strained like steel. . . .
> With growing zeal
> Year by year
> The industries flourished and grew. . . .

The boy was dozing. He could not keep his eyes open. Stupid, boring words that called up no images escaped his memory. I could not do anything to liven him up and make him learn, when he suddenly recalled something and his eyes sparkled.

'Mother, your shoes are falling to pieces, aren't they?'

'They are.' I showed him my shoes, burst in ten places, with the soles nearly off. I could not get a permit to buy cheap shoes because such permits could only be obtained through one's place of employment and I was despised at my office for my 'lack of interest in social work'. And I could not buy an ordinary pair or have one made because that would have cost about two hundred roubles, almost the whole of my salary for two months.

The boy ran to the kitchen and brought me in triumph a pair of worn but perfectly sound shoes.

'Where did you get them from?' I cried joyfully.

'Don't you remember? Last year you wanted to give them to that girl across the road, but they got stowed away behind the book-case instead. I found and cleaned them, so here's a present for you.'

'You darling! Why, they are lovely shoes.'

Cheering up he suddenly recited the poem at one breath, jumped into bed and, as he was dropping asleep, said dreamily:

'Mother, if you manage to get to the market to-morrow, will you buy me an egg? It is seventy copecks,* that's not too dear, is it?'

'I'll buy you two, but you must go to sleep.'

The boy fell asleep and I sat up by myself in the desolate half-empty flat ㅜ most of the furniture had been sold piece by piece. The sense of empty blankness descended upon me once more; I felt as though I were alone in the whole world. The houses, the streets, the town, seemed to vanish; there was only deep, unbroken darkness around me, and in the far, far distance a vague outline of the prison. In my mind I drew the walls apart and saw my husband's face as pale as it was during those minutes when we looked at each other for the last time. Was he still living?

* One and fivepence.

·

CHAPTER XI

TROUBLES at the office, endless struggles for every piece of bread, for every log of wood, for every moment of existence, are hard to bear at all times and become unendurable when the family is broken up and the threat of death hangs over it. But the succession of empty, depressing days held one bright spot – the day of taking parcels to the prisoners.

The parcels contained a change of linen and a specified quantity of food-stuffs, enumerated in the official list. One could not send a single word of greeting, no message of any description – not even to say that all at home were well. But for the prisoners this parcel, every detail of which reminded them of home, was their sole link with life; for their families, preparing the parcel was the only thing really worth doing. All the prisoners and their wives, mothers, children, lived for the 'parcel day' and looked forward to it as though it were a day of meeting.

One might think it was all quite simple – you collected the linen and the food, passed on the parcel, and that was all. But in truth it was by no means simple.

To begin with, you had to get the food-stuffs: meat, eggs, butter, apples, dried fruit, salted cucumbers, tobacco, tea, sugar. All these things could perhaps be bought at the shops for OGPU agents; ordinary

Co-ops hardly ever had them in stock, and then only in very small quantities – and for prison-parcels you had to have them every week. `

At home Soviet citizens feed on potatoes, flavouring them with herrings, onions, and any stray products that happen to find their way into the market. To find the rare food-stuffs needed for the parcels was rather like a task that witches set people in fairy tales. We could not have done it at all but for the wretched, dirty, free markets; the Soviet Government has had so far to tolerate small private dealers who often help the shop assistants to steal from the Co-ops. The prices on those markets were such that a parcel cost more than half of one's monthly salary, i.e., 60–70 roubles.* It was vexing to see what poor stuff that money bought: stale bits of meat, butter mixed with margarine, wizened apples, doubtful eggs. And to buy these things you had first to sell some of your remaining possessions. Clothes, clocks, books, crockery, furniture was sold for next to nothing; we had to break up our homes in order to keep alive the men whose hard work had once built them up.

Two days of anxious running about were barely sufficient to do the selling and the buying. It often happened, meanwhile, as though to spite us, that some tinned goods – fish, lobsters, etc., would be rejected for export, and, not being good enough for the 'European bourgeois' would be sold comparatively cheaply to Soviet citizens. Everyone rejoiced and feasted, but none of it could be sent to prison, for the articles in question were not mentioned in the official list of the OGPU. Only ordinary criminals could

* Since then prices of food-stuffs have increased.

receive almost anything; every time we went to the
prison office we read enviously the long list of things
allowed them.

Then it had all to be packed in one bag: underclothes, eggs, meat rissoles, apples, salted cucumbers,
tobacco, etc. The paper in which things were wrapped
had to be without any letters or signs on it, and cotton
bags containing tea and sugar could not be tied since
everything of the nature of string was strictly forbidden
in prison. Owing to the paper crisis the Co-ops did
not wrap up a single article, but simply weighed
things out loose in the scales; on the free market pur-
chases were wrapped up in old newspapers. Without a
special permit you could not buy paper in a shop. If in
packing the parcel you failed to observe one of the
rules, all the contents were thrown out and the prisoner
received nothing.

All this was difficult, but Soviet citizens, especially
women, are resourceful. The thought that everything
we had cooked and collected would be taken to the
prison and that our men were looking forward to it as
to a holiday, made everything seem easy; though I
admit that to obtain the right kind of paper we sometimes had to steal. The worst we had to go through was
outside the prison.

Parcels were accepted from nine in the morning, but
as I had to go to my work afterwards I had to be in the
queue quite early. I left home about seven, when it is
still quite dark in winter. The heavy bag kept slipping
out of my hands; the tram-car was packed. It was
damp and cold; everything one touched was wet and
dirty. I was so tired and sleepy that all my inside
seemed to be trembling. At the prison gates one had to

slip unobserved into the gateway of the house opposite. It is not forbidden to walk past the prison, but
if the sentry sees women with sacks he rudely drives
them away and threatens them with his rifle – there
must be no queue outside a prison, though their
sinister closed car rushes about the town collecting
victims day and night.

In the Butyrki Prison in Moscow things are far
worse. Many women there come in the evening and
spend the night in the porches of the neighbouring
houses: there are so many prisoners, and the queue is so
long that a woman who arrives by the first morning
car may be too late to give in her parcel that day. In
Petersburg the queue formed in the evil-smelling gateway. It consisted almost entirely of women, most of
them over forty and some quite sixty. Almost all were
of the educated class: wives of engineers, professors,
academicians. They were badly dressed: shabby overcoats, old hats, leaky shoes. All their better clothes
had been sold. All looked with anguish at the cruel
grey walls behind which were their nearest and
dearest.

What was happening to them? Were they alive? No
one could tell. . . . It was rumoured that at Butyrki
parcels brought by the parents for their son had been
accepted for a whole month after the young man had
been shot. When at last the prison authorities bestirred
themselves to notify the father and mother of his death,
the old people could not survive the shock and hanged
themselves. Here the other day, they shot a man by
mistake, because the prison-officer misread the name.
Other prisoners had read their own death sentence in
the papers, but were waiting for their turn, as there

were too many victims to be dispatched in the prison cellars.

We knew nothing about the fate of our men. Tired and cold, we stood there whispering.

'How long is it since your husband was taken?'

'It will soon be a month.'

'Oh, that's nothing! Mine has been here a year.'

'A year? How? Who has been here a year?' everyone was alarmed.

'Ah, yes, of course, he is an academician! Yes, yes!'

All were reassured. It was nothing new.

'And yours?'

'Three days.'

This one had quite a frightened look. She did not seem to have recovered since the night of the arrest. She was only about twenty. Her girlish face was plump and round.

'You know,' she could not resist telling us, 'Valya, my husband, came home in the evening and said, "you know, darling (she blushed at the word that escaped her), they are taking young men now, so you must be ready. Don't be alarmed." I did not believe him and took no notice of what he said, and in the night they came for him. I was so frightened that I have been trembling all over ever since.'

It certainly was rather like conscription in war-time, only they began with the old and ended with the young.

'I am afraid I don't know what to do,' she complained.

'Never mind, you will see for yourself when we go in,' I reassured her.

'But tell me, what have you put in your parcel?' someone asked sympathetically.

'Rusks.'

'That's good.'

'A lemon. . . .'

'No, no, you mustn't! Lemons are not allowed! Make haste, take out the lemon.' Everyone was alarmed as though something dreadful had happened.

'But why? Why may I send an apple and not a lemon?' she protested.

'You mayn't, you mayn't. It's not in the list. They'll throw away the whole of your parcel.'

Her hands trembled. The lemon could not be discovered in the big bag. She very nearly wept. Others helped her. At last the lemon was found. But now the whole list of the contents had to be re-copied, for no corrections in it were allowed.

'Never mind, we'll find some paper for you directly,' we comforted her.

We gave her paper and indelible pencil – almost everyone carried that in case of emergency. The girl had to write, but her hand was shaking. She tried to control herself, remembering that there must be no corrections or erasures on the list, but suddenly she dropped a big tear right on to the paper and made a big smudge.

'No, they won't accept it now, that official is a horrid man. Write it out again,' the others said in answer to her pitiful glance.

That was how we all had to be trained, and we did it all obediently, anxious not to anger the OGPU agents, who would make our dear ones suffer for it.

'I wish they'd make haste and open the doors,' said a tired, sick-looking woman.

'It is past nine.'

'I hope they won't be long, my feet are simply frozen.' There were about forty of us by now. There was very little room in the gateway and we could no longer stand one behind the other. We were tired; our bags seemed heavy and we could not put them down anywhere – it was wet snow and mud underfoot.

'We can go in!' someone in front cried joyfully. The prison gates opposite were slowly opening. We all ran across the road. It was light by now. People were going to work. Free men. . . . And our husbands? What was awaiting them – death or forced labour?

The room where parcels were given in was small. Its two windows had iron bars; the panes were so dirty that they looked like greased paper. The hanging lamp with a white shade was covered with thick black flakes of dust. The grime on the walls and ceiling completely obliterated their original colour. The air was stale and sour. Every day from morning till three in the afternoon the room was crowded and it was never ventilated, not even in the summer. There was nowhere to sit down – not a single chair or bench, and so all leaned against the filthy walls. There was a wooden partition across the room and in it two openings closed with shutters. Behind the partition were those on whom our joy or grief depended that day – OGPU agents in charge of the transfer of parcels. We stood and waited again.

In front of me stood a nun, thin but well-made and strong, and a pale, grey-haired, elegant-looking old lady. She was trembling with nervousness and muttering like one insane.

'Forty years, forty years . . .'

'Forty years of what?' I asked.

'We've lived together for forty years. . . . Good God, what is it for, what is it for? . . . He is an architect. You know him, don't you? Everyone knows him.'

Yes, thought I, that was true. So much the worse for him, his name might be useful to the OGPU.

'I know,' I said. 'He created a whole school. His text-books are used everywhere.'

'There, you see,' she said joyfully. 'Surely, they can't shoot a man like that? If you only knew how he worked, day and night. Why, why did they take him?'

I said nothing. All were silent. Why did they take all the others?

Only two or three ladies chattered. Their husbands were dentists. Those are imprisoned simply to wring money out of them. If they have not any, they are kept longer, but on the whole, are released fairly soon.

It was getting on to ten o'clock. The room was crowded, the last arrivals were standing outside, but the windows in the partition were still closed.

'How much longer will they be? They should open at nine?' all said in timid whispers.

At last the windows opened noisily. An OGPU official could be seen sitting at the table, a box with a card-index of names in front of him. His face looked quite wooden, as in a caricature: low forehead with a dent in the middle into which the peak of his cap seemed to fit.

He roughly seized the paper handed him by the nun: the name was written at the top, then followed the list of contents of the parcel. He spent a long time fumbling in the card-index. The men behind him were sorting out bags with the return parcels of soiled linen. There was a smell of disinfectants and a sour smell of dirty clothes. The official was laughing and talking to some-one, forgetting the name, beginning to look for it again. We all stood with beating hearts: would the parcel be accepted? . . . It was the one thing that mattered at the moment.

He underlined the name with a blue pencil, wrote down the number of the cell and threw back the list to the nun.

'It's accepted,' she sighed joyfully, crossed herself secretly and went to the second window.

'Next!'

The poor grey-haired lady, trembling, gave him her list crumpled by her nervous hands. He immedi-ately flung it back to her.

'There's no such man here.'

'How do you mean? Where is he, then? Where?'

'I tell you, he isn't here.'

'But they told me he was here, I inquired at the OGPU headquarters,' she said breathlessly, gasping with agitation.

'Citizen, go away!' the flat-headed OGPU agent roared menacingly. 'The next!'

'But where is he? Where?' the old lady cried in despair, beating her head against the window-frame.

'Go away or you'll be led out,' the man growled.

We led the poor woman aside, soothing her, advising her in which prison she had better look for her husband – Kresty, Nizhegorodsky or Gorohovy. Everyone was afraid that *he* might be angry. Though officially he is supposed to do no more than look up the names in the card-index, we all fancied that the permission to give in the parcel depended upon his good or bad will. And as a matter of fact a good deal did depend upon him.

For instance, for two weeks in succession he drove away a mother who could not discover her son, a boy of eighteen, in any prison, though he had been arrested. When at last she fainted on the spot, we all begged him to look through the card-index once more; he did, and found the boy's name right enough.

'The cards had stuck together,' he said airily. 'Well, citizen, give in your parcel.'

But the citizen had first to be restored to life. To spend a fortnight looking for one's son in OGPU offices and prisons, fearing that perhaps he had already been shot, was enough to drive anyone to despair – and all through the carelessness of an official of whom it is no use to complain.

And so the queue moved on: two or three were refused and walked away distressed and bewildered, others were allowed to give their parcels in and felt happy as on Easter Day. Only some twenty-five per cent of the prisoners receive parcels, others have to live on prison rations, without a change of linen, without any link with their home; it is like being buried alive. When parcels are forbidden it means that the examining officer is 'putting pressure' on the prisoner, trying to wear him out. It is a bad sign.

When permission had been given at the first window, things were easier at the second, though there, too, there was some risk because the second OGPU man also wanted to exercise his power.

'Why is your bag wet?'

'Because it's raining.'

'I shan't accept it next time.'

That was how he went on about every trifle. Tears and entreaties were of no use – his decisions were irrevocable. If peasant women came, they fared worst of all: they could not be made to observe the rules, and OGPU is equally cruel to all.

'Citizen Ivanov!'

'Yes, brother' . . . an old woman in huge felt-boots and a sheepskin coat, her head wrapped in a shawl, made her way through the crowd.

'Why did you put a newspaper in? I can't accept your parcel.'

'Why, brother, it's not for reading, it's just to make into cigarettes, only half a sheet. We can't read or write; we are country-people. Have pity, brother!'

'Citizen, take away your parcel!' and the sack was flung back. The old woman wept and entreated, ready to fall at the man's feet, but the burly official, who probably himself had come from the country and had a mother like this old woman, would not even look at her. He did not care whom he drove away – an illiterate old peasant or a little boy, left fatherless and motherless, as perhaps my son would be soon.

And so every week there was this secret joy bought at the cost of humiliation before the unbridled brutality of those who carry out 'the dictatorship of the proletariat'.

·

CHAPTER XII

A TRYING DAY

IT was in February, 1931. The morning was just as usual. It was dark. It was difficult to get up. I felt sick of work and could hardly drag myself to my office. It was more than four months since my husband's arrest; he might be sentenced any day. There seemed to be fewer death sentences, but crowds were sent to forced labour in the penal camps. I could not help thinking of every trifle as a bad omen, and this time, as I came out on to the landing, I saw a large, half-frozen pool of blood. It must have been my drunken neighbour stumbling and damaging his nose as he came home in the night, but my heart sank and I kept seeing red patches on the snow-covered streets all the way.

I did not know in those days that OGPU shoots its victims in the cellars and not in the prison courtyard.

No sooner had I settled down to my work than my colleague at the Hermitage ran into my room.

'Do you know, Mrs. Engelhardt* has killed herself. Her husband has been sentenced to ten years penal servitude at Solovki. When she heard this she threw herself down from the top landing. You remember, he was arrested in connection with the academicians' case.

* Sister of the well-known writer, Garshin. Her husband was one of the keepers of the Pushkinsky Dom museum.

Mrs. Engelhardt, whose lovely hair was almost too heavy for her head – so it was she who had been lying in a pool of blood!

An hour afterwards I found that instead of working I was rocking myself to and fro and repeating: 'What are we coming to? What are we coming to?'

It was clear enough though – total extermination of the educated class in Russia.

It was more than a year since Platonov and others on the staff of the Academy of Science had been imprisoned; more than six months since the arrest of the Moscow professors of history, four months since the arrest of the remaining assistants at the *Pushkinsky Dom* Museum. Besides, numbers of people were arrested in between and, if they had any relation to literature or publishing, were included in the 'academicians' case' – even though they had never met Platonov or any of the historians. The OGPU had been cooking up the case for over a year, but were not able to present it to the public. They had evidently been given the task of discrediting scholars who held an independent point of view, of proving their connection with the emigrés, of frightening the working class with the bogey of 'intervention' and 'monarchist conspiracy' and providing sensational material for foreign propaganda. The 'academicians' case' was to have been tried publicly, but the evidence was faked to such an extent that an open trial would have been unwise: two many famous scholars were involved, and it might alienate public opinion abroad – which the Politbureau to some extent considers. The death sentence, usual in such cases, was talked of all the time; but it would have produced a bad impression on foreigners. On the other hand, it would damage the OGPU officials' career to confess that no trace of the alleged conspiracy, in which more than 200 people were implicated, could be discovered. Angry that the Government was going to deprive them of a sensational trial, the OGPU, to preserve its dignity, decided to wind up the case on the quiet. Breaking up the accused into groups, it shot those whose names were not too well known, sentenced others to ten years penal servitude, sending them off to the camps in groups of thirty or forty. Very few were sentenced to five years, and only the 'leaders', men of European fame – whose fate hung in the balance for another six months – were given five years 'free exile', that is, were banished to obscure provincial towns. No one thought that in spite of the campaign of terror the OGPU would be allowed to deal so cruelly with men whose only guilt could have been lack of interest in politics. It was no wonder that the shock was too much for the wives. Life becomes unbearable when there is nothing but senseless cruelty all round.

At home I heard another piece of news.

'Professor Butenko's wife has hanged herself.'

'Why?'

'Her husband has been sentenced to ten years penal servitude in connection with the "academicians" case'. All their property is confiscated. The OGPU agents came to make the inventory. She asked them to wait a minute, went to her room and hanged herself. By the time they grew tired of waiting for her and broke the door she was already dead.'

'She did it just in time. . . .'

'Yes, it's a pity her husband did not. He doesn't yet

know that their daughter is dead. His wife concealed it from him, though she was allowed to see him once since then. He won't last long now.'

'No, he won't.'

And, indeed, when he heard the news of his wife's and daughter's death he fell seriously ill and died at the penal camp at Solovki.

I do not know whether anyone had told him what touching care his daughter, a girl of sixteen, took of him while he was in prison. After his arrest she kept the family by selling their belongings, looked after her mother, who quite lost her head with grief, wore herself out taking parcels to prison. When she caught typhoid her heart was too weak to fight the disease. In her delirium she talked of her father and worried about one thing only. She kept saying, 'Tell me, when is Sunday? Mother must not forget about the parcel. How dreadful that I am ill! Mother does not know how strict they are in prison. She is sure to make some mistake, and they won't take the parcel. Daddy, darling daddy, what will become of you?'

Poor child! Her life too was centred on the prison, the bags with linen and food and the fear of the OGPU. She died thinking of it. Her mother had followed her. It was her father's turn now.

Some months later I heard that the wife of the academician Lazarev had hanged herself, learning that her husband had been sentenced to ten years penal servitude. Two months after her death the OGPU commuted his sentence to exile; they wanted to make use of his name as an advertisement for science in U.S.S.R.

Three victims! . . . And how many more there were,

obscure and unknown! . . . There was nothing surprising in the fact that the wives of professors, academicians and other specialists should want to die rather than witness the horrible fate of their husbands, for whom they could do nothing.

Suicide is a selfish action, but it may be an indication of the general state of things: when there is nothing to live for and no strength to carry on, there is nothing left but death.

CHAPTER XIII

'ORDER FOR SEARCH AND ARREST'

IT happened on a Saturday in March. It had been a good day – the day of giving in parcels. And the evening, too, had been peaceful. I wanted to go to bed, but the boy's knickers were torn and I had to patch them up so that he could wear them in the morning; he had only one pair. I finished my work about one in the morning when there was a loud ring at the bell. I opened the door: the house-porter and two OGPU agents in military uniform stood before me.

So this was the end.

I had kept hoping it would not happen. It was so dreadful to think that my husband would be left without any help in prison and my little boy alone with strangers.

I had made several attempts to arrange for someone to take care of him in case I were arrested. But *all* my husband's friends were shot, and all my friends were being imprisoned one after another. Three people who had promised to take charge of my son were arrested in succession, and I did not dare to ask for help any more. Besides, I knew that it would not be safe for anyone to give a home to the child, for people were frequently arrested for assisting the families of those who were already in prison. In a case of a certain family that I knew *twenty* persons were imprisoned for helping them.

My poor, darling, rosy boy, how could I go away from you, leaving you alone in the night! I think death will be easier than was that parting with the child. . . .

I could hardly stand on my feet, but I had to control myself – I was not going to break down before the OGPU men. We went into the room. The senior OGPU agent gave me a pinkish paper, 'Order for search and arrest.'

'Please.'

The house-porter stood there in silence, looking away. He was an old man; he was sorry for me and ashamed to be present at the final break up of my home. The younger OGPU agent eagerly looked about him, not venturing yet to set to work – like a dog who has not yet been told 'fetch it'. As soon as his senior got up he rushed into the boy's room.

'That's my son's room. Perhaps you'll leave him in peace for the moment and begin here. It will be more convenient for you,' I added, seeing that they hesitated.

They gave in sullenly and in silence.

The senior agent motioned me to a chair by my desk and began turning out the drawers, while the other tackled the bookcase. Neither of them spoke. With cinematographic rapidity the room was reduced to a state of indescribable chaos. No Soviet propaganda picture of 'a search in 1905' could equal it.

One after the other the books were chucked out of the bookcase. Dante, Petrarch, Boccaccio – objects of my youthful enthusiasm; Rousseau, Voltaire, Delille – but those were in too many volumes, so only some of them were picked out. What joy it had been to discover at some second-hand book shop old editions in fine leather bindings! On the lower shelves stood valuable illustrated books – landmarks of years gone by. The OGPU agent flung them open, breaking the backs, and chucked them on the sofa, from which they slid on to the floor. He probably thought that books existed for the sole purpose of hiding money or letters in them.

The turn of music came next. They opened the top of the piano and books of music fell on the floor, breaking up into separate leaves.

The other man was busy with the shelves containing my card-index. Cards with various quotations and references, collected in the course of many years and carefully sorted out according to subjects in alphabetical order, flew on to the table and were scattered on the floor – white, blue, yellow. The intricate work of a lifetime was instantly transformed into meaningless rubbish. Soon the floor was littered to such an extent that one could hardly step on it, but the agent's eye fell on my work-basket with rags and undarned stockings. Opening the lid the smart-looking OGPU man said to me scornfully:

'Turn it out.'

I threw the rags and the stockings on top of the books and papers. Let them amuse themselves! The longer this senseless business goes on the better – I need not wake the boy as yet. He was asleep and little knew what awaited him.

The OGPU agents might chuck things about and spoil them as much as they liked. The only pity was that it all went on the floor and not straight into the fire. I would have liked to burn everything, just as my love for home, and books, and work was burning to ashes in my heart. To the devil with all our culture! So long as Russia is ruled by the OGPU no one wants it, and it only leads people to prison and exile.

The devastation was complete. I had to wake the child.

My darling boy, with candid friendly eyes, how hard it was to wake you!

He did not in the least want to wake up. I kissed him, caressed him, but he closed his eyes and turned away, not understanding what I wanted of him. But OGPU hasn't much patience: the men waited for a minute and then burst into the room. The boy turned pale with fright in his sleep and woke up.

'Mother, are they taking you too?'

'Yes, darling.'

He did not weep or complain. He only clung to me, throwing his soft little arms round my neck, and watching with frightened eyes the OGPU agent rummaging in his table, among his ink-stained copybooks.

'Get ready, quick.'

Disentangling myself with difficulty from the boy, I began collecting a change of linen in the chest of drawers that had been turned inside out.

'Sign the protocol.'

I signed the statement that nothing had been taken from me during the search, and that I had no complaints to make.

'Call your neighbour and ask her to take charge of the boy.'

He must have known that I had no one to turn to. My neighbour came to live in the flat after my

husband's arrest, when it was very painful for me to
meet fresh people, and I did not know her at all.

'Come along.'

That was the end. I kissed the child for the last time,
walked for the last time through the devastated rooms,
stepping on the books and the music, looked for the
last time at the light in my windows.

How one has the strength to go through it all, I
don't know.

In the streets stood the closed prison car, a gloomy-
looking contrivance. Big, empty, completely closed,
with narrow benches along the sides, it resembled the
van for homeless dogs caught in the streets at daybreak. It shook, rattled, dived, as it were, among waves
of stone, because snow was being cleared from the
streets and frozen lumps lay in heaps everywhere.
The noise, the jolting, the piercing shrieks of the
hooter made one sick and giddy. At last we stopped. I
could hear the gates open; the car drove into the prison
courtyard.

It was a sinister place, surrounded by tall, dark
buildings. A dirty gloomy staircase, worn down by
the warders' heavy boots, a door behind iron bars, the
impudently staring faces of the keepers, bad, sour air
smelling of stale tobacco – it all was hideous, but I no
longer cared. A dull calm descended upon me: prison
was before me, and there was no going back.

I was told to sit down on a bench in the office. A fat
OGPU agent sat at the table, yawning and picking his
nose. A sleepy dishevelled young woman with painted
lips, manicured nails and ink-stained fingers, was
yawning at another table. They were both sleepy and
had not the energy to tackle me. It must have been

very boring for them: the same thing every night, and so many times in the night, too!

Ten minutes passed, twenty. It would soon be three in the morning. At last the fat man bestirred himself and gave me a questionnaire to fill up. Nothing is done without a questionnaire in U.S.S.R.

I filled it up and sat there again, waiting – or perhaps no longer waiting for anything.

The clock struck three. The OGPU clerks were dozing. Another ten minutes passed. So many useless minutes, and at home they hurried me so. . . . It is always like this in prison: everyone is expected to obey orders instantly, but the authorities waste hours which mount up to months and years.

At twenty minutes past three the fat man stretched his arm lazily to the telephone receiver. . . . I had been sitting there for over an hour already.

'Are you ready? . . . Directly.'

He yawned, sat down again, had a smoke, and getting up heavily pointed to the door into the corridor. There with a lazy gesture he handed me over to the sleepy warder. We walked on, I in front and he behind, directing me from time to time:

'Downstairs.'

'To the left.'

'To the right.'

It was a hideous sensation – to walk hearing behind me the steps of the warder who drove me down dirty stairs and corridors that grew narrower and darker as we went on. On the ground floor I suddenly lost my self-control: senseless, panic fear possessed me so completely that for a moment I saw dark. There was nothing terrifying before me: a long, dirty corridor with a black asphalt floor, along the wall a thick pipe of the central heating that made a low humming sound – that was all. And yet horror of prison, of death – not for myself, but for my husband and perhaps my abandoned child, suddenly overwhelmed me, and I had an immediate sensation of how huge the prison was.

'Left!'

We entered a low, cool corridor. A ventilation-pane must have been opened somewhere. My heart began to beat more evenly and I felt normal once more.

Another staircase and I was brought into a curious place. At the bottom there was an asphalt court; on the right a blank wall three stories high; on the left – three tiers of galleries, like hanging iron balconies communicating by means of iron stairs. The iron doors of solitary confinement cells, set deeply in the wall opened on to the galleries. Above the iron ceiling in which there was an opening for the stairs there were two more stories. The massive walls were painted the colour of lead; everything else was iron.

Dead stillness reigned in this sinister place. Electric light had been put out and an oil lamp was burning dimly on a little table. The warder on duty in soft slippers walked noiselessly to meet me. He silently dismissed my escort and said in a stern whisper:

'Take off your coat.'

I took it off; he examined it.

'Your hat, your galoshes, your shoes.'

He examined these too.

But at that moment I again lost my head for a moment. A woman had noiselessly walked up to me from behind; I could barely hear her steps. When she was beside me I instinctively turned round to look at her. In the dim light of the kerosene lamp I saw her head tied with a bright red handkerchief with the Soviet emblem over the forehead, and her pale face without a nose. At the same instant this woman passed her hands over the whole of my body so shamelessly that I almost fainted with horror and repulsion.

Later on I learned that this woman was one of our best wardresses. She had been a prostitute all her life, and when she had ruined her health she took a post in the prison. She was rough and often swore at the prisoners in her nasal voice, but she was kind to them in her simple-hearted way. She spied on us in so far as it formed part of her duties, but without special zeal; she dealt with offences against discipline at her own discretion and did not complain to the superior officers about every trifle. But I grew to appreciate all this only much later. That night her deformed face encircled by a red Soviet kerchief seemed to me a symbolic mask of evil and corruption with which the Soviet prison greeted me.

I heard the rattle of the key in an iron lock. The door of the cell opened heavily, letting me in and immediately shut behind me. The key was turned three times and all was still. I was in the cell at last. It was high time. I was very nearly fainting with fatigue.

·

CHAPTER XIV

A BAD NIGHT

THE cell was cold and damp. Water was dripping from the frozen window high up in the wall, and the asphalt floor was wet as after rain. The straw mattress on the iron bedstead was damp and dirty. Mustering my courage I made my bed and lay down in my clothes, covering myself with my overcoat. I wanted to shut my eyes and see nothing.

There was another woman in the cell. She lay on a bed by the door. When I was brought in she did not stir beneath her magnificent fur coat, from under which I could see only her lace night-cap.

It seemed strange – the hideous, smelly cell and these furs and lace. But people are brought into prison just as they are; it is only in the concentration camps that all are reduced to the same dead level.

When the warder walked away from the 'peep-hole', satisfied that I was not going to do anything desperate, my neighbour raised her head and looked at me attentively. I saw a young and very beautiful woman. Her face was so pale and thin, her big, dark-rimmed eyes were so full of sorrow that she looked like an actress made up for the last act of a tragedy.

'When?' she asked in a whisper, addressing me as though we had known each other for years. Prison brings people closer together than any friendship.

'Just now.'

'And I've been here exactly a year.'

'A year?' I sat up to look at her.

'Yes, a year to a day. It is bad luck for you to have been put into my cell.'

I stared at her and did not venture to say anything. A year of prison, a year in this horrid, damp, stinking cell! How had she survived it? And did she think I, too, would have a year of it?

'Your husband is in prison?' she asked confidently.

'Yes.'

'Is he an engineer?'

'No. He is a scientist, a University professor.'

'Mine is an engineer. Has your husband been in prison long?'

'Four months.'

'You took parcels to him in prison? Tried to intercede for him? Applied to Moscow?' she asked, with a kind of malice.

'Yes.'

'I too. We oughtn't to have done it. *They* don't like it.'

'The OGPU, you mean?'

'Yes. Now your husband is done for, and you too. We are wretched fools, that's what we are.'

'But could we have done anything different?'

'No, we couldn't.'

She spoke no more and lay down. The shutter over the 'peep-hole' rustled slightly; an unfriendly eye scrutinised us intently. She pretended to sleep, but as soon as the footsteps died away she resumed the conversation.

'Have you any children?'

'One boy.'

'I too. Whom have you left yours with?'

'Alone. The people living in our flat are mere acquaintances,' I said miserably, dreading to think of how he was feeling alone in the night for the first time in his life.

'Mine is with his granny, but she is seventy. I can't think what they are doing. My God! My God! A whole year. What they are living on, how they manage to exist – I know nothing, nothing at all!'

We were silent: both were choking with tears. In prison one must not think about one's children, must not recall their dear little faces with frightened eyes – it is unbearable.

Tears slowly trickled down her cheeks, but her face remained fixed like a mask.

'We ought to die,' she said decidedly, almost aloud.

'Why?'

'We did not watch over our children. We ought to have deserted our husbands at once for the sake of the children. Now *they* will destroy us all.'

She always said 'they' instead of the OGPU. It was like the Fate of the Greek tragedies, inexorable and remorseless.

'But why would it be better for them if we died?' I asked indignantly. I had always imagined that I was essential for my son's happiness, but my neighbour spoke with such conviction that her judgment seemed final.

'It would be much better. They would be orphans then. A father and mother like us are simply a millstone round a child's neck.'

Perhaps she was right. I recalled that children of

men sent to penal servitude have difficulty in finishing
the secondary school and are not allowed to go on to
the Universities. If they become factory-hands they
are not allowed to specialise, but must always remain
unskilled workers. It is all very well for Krupskaya to
write that all children have a right to be educated;
words do not commit her to anything, and her name
is an excellent advertisement for naïve people. The
children of the '48' who were shot were expelled from
everywhere, even from classes of foreign languages.
Perhaps our children really would be better off if we
died and the OGPU forgot about us.

'I have tried,' she went on in a calm, businesslike
voice.

'Tried what?'

'To die. Three times.'

'Yes, and what happened?'

'I haven't succeeded, but I will; one must only have
patience.'

Her face was calm, her eyes were intelligent, and yet
she talked in this wild way.

'It is difficult to cut one's veins,' she continued. 'One
cannot get enough warm water and blood congeals.
I cut myself very thoroughly and lost no end of blood,
but I didn't die; I only grew very weak.'

'What did you do it with?' I asked, adopting her tone
in spite of myself.

'Glass. I broke the window-pane. I still keep a few
pieces by me, in case.' She fumbled for the pieces of
glass hidden inside her mattress.

'To hang oneself is very difficult – they watch me;
but once I very nearly did it.'

As I listened to her I felt that she was introducing

me to a new, special world, created by the prison, and
our conversation no longer seemed mad to me.

'I asked for some bandages, twisted them into a rope,
tied it to the lavatory tank, put the halter round my
neck and jumped off the seat. I quite enjoyed it at the
moment.'

'Yes?'

'My neighbour woke up when I began to choke. I am
very tall, and I suppose my feet got in the way when
I lost consciousness so that I did not die at once,' she
said with annoyance. 'But it's very horrid.'

'What is horrid?'

'The coming to. Usually they carry people to the
hospital, but they thought I was dead already, so they
threw me down on the floor, just as I was in my shift.'

'Where?'

'Just at the bottom of the stairs, where the warder
on duty sits.'

That was the place where I was so foolishly frightened of the noseless wardress. Now I was listening to
something really frightening, but I no longer minded.
I asked her where she hanged herself.

'In this cell. Over there,' she pointed to the lavatory
tank to which she had fixed the rope.

So evidently it was the same in prison as out of it –
only here death was not so easy.

'The thing is to starve oneself to death,' she went on.
'That's the most certain of all.'

'Why, do they allow it?'

'Oh, that's all right. I starved for twenty days before
they noticed it. They are afraid of hunger-strikes in
common cells, but here I was alone. I used to pour the
food down the drain. But one day they called me to the

examining officer and I was too weak to walk. Then
there was a lot of fuss. They dragged me to the hospital,
the doctors took no end of trouble and pulled me
through. But you can't think how nice wine tastes
after fasting!' she added, with sudden animation. 'A
tiny glassful is as good as a bottle of champagne.'

There was a spark of long-forgotten gaiety in her
eyes.

'I did enjoy having a good time, sinner that I am!
But surely there's nothing wrong in that? My husband
worked day and night, they themselves paid him
thousands, and now they ask where did we get the
money from, why did we twice have dinner at the
Hotel d'Europe! Damned hypocrites! They fling
money about, open expensive restaurants – and then
we have to pay with our lives for having had a bit of
fun. "Bribery by foreign capitalists", indeed! Why, I've
never set eyes on one. I only read about them in
English novels. No, I cannot endure this any longer.
They have promised me to let me see my son; I'll have
a last look at him and die. My heart will not stand
another long fast.'

'Is it painful to starve?'

'No, only the first days. Afterwards one just feels
weak, and only half awake. And one has such nice
dreams: freedom, real life, my own precious darling
boy. Ah, if they'd let me out I would live for him
alone.'

'But perhaps they will let you out. Your case must
end some day.'

'No,' she said sternly. 'You don't know *them*. *They*
won't let me out because I'd rather die than tell the
lie they want me to tell.'

Towards morning I got warm under my coat and dozed off. I dreamt that I was at home, that I had dropped asleep on the sofa and had forgotten to put out the lamp I put out my hand to do it, and woke up with the cold.

'What is it?' my neighbour asked. She was sitting on her bed and looking at me attentively. Days and nights were merged for her into one blank succession of moments to which there was no end.

'The light. I dreamt that I had forgotten to put out the lamp.'

'They don't put it out in my cell; they are afraid of what I might do. Sleep, they'll take you to the examining officer to-morrow.'

But I could not go to sleep any more. In my dream I had had for the last time a feeling of home, and waking up I understood that my home was lost for ever.

CHAPTER XV

THE EXAMINING OFFICER

I WENT calmly to my first interview with the examining officer. I imagined that it would be business-like, and might help to clear matters. Though my arrest was a sure sign that my husband's position had changed for the worse, I naively imagined that I could be useful to him by confirming his innocence. It never occurred to me that the sole object of my arrest was to force him to confess something he had never done. I learned afterwards that the examining officer had confronted him with the dilemma of either signing the statement that he was a 'wrecker' or of being the cause of my arrest. Nor did I know at the time that after my arrest my husband was presented with another alternative: either he must confess his 'guilt' or he would be shot, I would get ten years penal servitude and our son be sent to a colony for homeless children. I knew that wives were often arrested on their husbands' account, but I had no idea that the OGPU so shamelessly used them as pawns in the game.

And so I confronted the examining officer with the naïveté of a 'free' woman. He was a youngish man; his face had a noncommittal expression, as official as his OGPU uniform. He did not say good morning or offer me to sit down. Later on I found out that OGPU manners fall into three categories: drily-formal, like those of the man I was meeting now; hysterically-threatening like those of the second official I had to deal with, and caressingly-polite. I did not come across the third variety, but I have been told that that was the most disgusting of all, especially for women. Having once adopted a particular style they do not vary it, and become as stereotyped as bad provincial actors on the stage. I do not know if any of them are sufficiently intelligent to behave differently, but probably this is not necessary: their decisions are settled beforehand and no special subtlety is required of them. To be clever and well-informed would be a needless luxury in investigating made-up cases.

The examination began by the question.

'Your social origin?'

'My father was a University professor. He was the son of a peasant and had nobility conferred on him on receiving his degree.'

'So you belong to the nobility?'

'Nobility conferred on individuals was not hereditary. My father was known well enough. You can look up his biography in the Encyclopædia.'

That particular official did not bother me any more about this point, but the next man I had to deal with made a fearful scene. He shouted that I was concealing my social origin, that I obviously did belong to the nobility, that I was a typical class-enemy, and so on. Surprised by his shouting, I said calmly but maliciously:

'Nobility conferred on individuals is not a class characteristic. We are typical intellectuals of democratic origin. At present you are treating intellectuals worse than the real gentry. If you like to consider me as belonging to the nobility, you are welcome to do so. I don't care.'

'Aha! You have confessed!' he suddenly yelled in triumph.

I was so surprised that I said nothing, but this incident made me understand how 'confessions' may be engineered, and how stupid of me it was to enter into an argument. Every extra word one says may be dangerous, and one must learn to be silent.

The first examining officer went on with the usual questions.

'Have you been in prison before?'

'No.'

According to a popular Soviet joke every official questionnaire ought to contain the questions: 'Have you been in prison before? If not, why not?'

'Have you been tried?'

'No.'

I saw that in writing down my answer he made a mistake in spelling. He must have caught a gleam of mockery in my eyes, and that served me a good turn: he let me write down my answers myself, which is allowed but seldom, especially to women. In their version the officials always manage to twist one's answers in the way they want.

'What visitors have you been having lately?'

'None of our friends have come to see us, and you know our relations from the questionnaire.'

My answer caused the examining officer to make a few edifying remarks.

'Let me tell you that the Soviet Government is severe but just. We know how to value people who are candid with us, but we do not hesitate to apply other measures to those who are not. You have a son. You might consider him.'

This phrase is said to all women who have children, but it always sounds like spiteful mockery. What can we do for our children now? Perhaps, indeed, the best thing we could do would be to die so as not to stand in their way.

'I want you to talk of your own accord. . . .'

'I do not know what the charge against me is and cannot tell what would be of interest to you,' I answered in the most correct tone of voice, growing more and more uneasy.

Questioned very closely, I maintained that I knew nothing about my husband's case, but I had to admit that one of the '48' who were shot, a friend of my husband's, came to see us a year or eighteen months before his arrest.

Alas, I knew many people exiled to Siberia and Solovki, because their friends who were afterwards arrested happened to call on them; whole families were banished to the remotest parts of the country simply because they had relatives abroad. Everyone in U.S.S.R. may be a source of danger to others, and there is no way of protecting oneself.

There was nothing surprising in my being regarded as a 'class-enemy', and yet I could not believe that even on OGPU logic I deserved Solovki. And so I naïvely asked whether the OGPU had taken into consideration that ever since the Revolution I had had work of my own and just before my arrest had been engaged on an important and responsible job.

The examining officer smiled condescendingly.

'That is of no interest to us,' he said.

That was a good comment on the claim that in U.S.S.R. a woman can have an independent position. We were obviously returning to the days of Ivan the Terrible, when families used to be exterminated root and branch.

When I was led back to my cell I very nearly collided with a most unpleasant individual who rushed out of a side door. A puny, crumpled-looking little man with a greyish, twitching face, he might have been cast for the part of Smerdyakov in the *Brothers Karamazov*.

'Water!' he shouted.

Through the open door I saw an elderly woman, obviously of the educated class. In a fit of hysterics she was banging her head against the table. Her glasses helplessly swayed to and fro on a thin black string. The door was quickly shut again, but I understood something more about the technique of cross-examinations.

A few days later I, too, was brought before 'Smerdyakov'.

This time I was led into a big room that was probably used for meetings. There was a massive carved oak table with a huge ornamental inkstand and an armchair to match, but it all looked dusty and untidy. The examining officer ran in after me, flung himself into the armchair, and began to toss about like a mad monkey.

'Spy!' he shouted, piercing me with his nasty, furtive eyes. I suppose, according to his programme, I ought to have turned deadly pale or blushed, but I was merely surprised.

'Yes, yes, spy!' he shouted, still louder, to be more

convincing. 'You were in communication with foreign capitalists, yes?'

I should have been much embarrassed if I had had to answer all the idiotic accusations which he showered at me, but apparently his aim was simply to overwhelm me with shouts, gestures and looks. It is beyond my power to describe that wild stream of abuse and threats.

'We shoot spies, we shoot them! We don't pity them! A bullet costs only seven copecks! I'll shoot you myself! Yes, myself, my dear little citizen,' he added in a caressing whisper. 'With this very hand,' he added, displaying a horrid, dirty, twitching hand and a dirty cuff.

I felt disgusted, but not in the least frightened, because it was too theatrical.

'I've been doing it for nine years. Oh, you don't like that? Never mind, you'll get used to it. We'll make friends yet, you and I! You'll talk to me nicely one day! I like people to speak to me candidly!'

I sat there utterly stupefied by all this hideous nonsense; I only knew that I must take as little notice of it as possible. I had heard before that examining officers have a way of shouting and swearing, but I did not know that they began by it.

'Well?' he stopped suddenly and almost lay across the table so as to look at me more closely.

'It's all such nonsense,' I said unexpectedly for myself, sadly and with sudden sincerity. I was thinking that shouts and threats were a professional method of intimidation, but that after all there was nothing to prevent him from carrying out any of his threats.

'What!' He nearly jumped off his chair. 'So that's the way you speak to me! We are hoity-toity, are we? Very well! I've broken better people than you, and you may be certain I'll bring you to your knees! I know the lot of you, you scurvy intellectuals! Injured innocence, righteous indignation! You do know how to give yourselves airs! And then you crawl on your belly and whine. You ought to be crushed, the whole pack of you, crushed like lice!' he suddenly yelled in an unnatural voice, clicking his dirty nail on the table with an expressive gesture, 'Like this, like this!'

I tried to distract my thoughts by examining the ink-stand and guessing what metal it was made of, and so on – anything to keep my attention from words which were merely intended to exasperate me.

'And your husband is a nice one! A professor, a scientist! To the devil with your science! I spit upon your science!'

He bit off the wet end of the cigarette he had in his mouth and expressively spat on the floor.

'There! We can do without you! Shoot you, and that's all about it.'

He carried on like this from nine in the evening till midnight. I heard nothing from him but threats and abuse – no questions, no definite charges.

After this séance of intimidation my cell seemed to me an abode of peace, the grating of the key in the lock – a lullaby. Broken with fatigue and disgust I lay there, unable either to sleep, or to think, with a sense of utter hopelessness: if this was called 'investigation', what sentence could my husband and I expect? So far I had managed to control myself

H

and had not said anything indiscreet, but it was clear that a prisoner was not regarded as a human being and his whole fate depended on the whim of the OGPU.

.

CHAPTER XVI

ANOTHER CROSS-EXAMINATION

'So here you are! Good day, sit down! How are you?'
'Very well, thank you.'

'Very well? You are laughing? And will you laugh much longer?'

'Till you do away with me,' I answered, adopting his tone.

'You won't have long to wait, not long,' the amiable official thundered again. 'Seven copecks is not much of an expense, and as to yourself . . . such a worker as you is not much of a loss, either.'

On the whole, however, the conversation – one could hardly call it a cross-examination – was 'on a cheerful note'.

This time we were in a small and comparatively clean room. Through the window I could see the sky, blue in the evening light. Branches still bare but pliant with the warmth of spring, rustled against the window-panes. Behind the window, spring was coming, there were people who could look freely at the boundless sky, and here . . . what more would one have to go through before being shot? Death did not frighten me, it was too disgusting to live like that. But the preliminaries were revolting. Where would they drag me? To what nasty things should I have to listen? They would put a sack over my head and shoot me from behind. Or would there be no sack? One would not even see the sky before dying.

'Are you dreaming? And what are you going to tell me about your dear husband?'

'What do you wish to know?'

'What I wish to know! Ha-ha-ha! Everything! Start away, I like to hear stories.'

He lit a cigarette and lolled back in his armchair. He was silent and I was silent too. I looked at the window – that was pleasant, anyway.

'Well?'

'Yes?'

'Move on! I haven't called you here to smoke cigarettes with you.'

He alone was smoking, of course.

'Question me.'

'I am not going to, you must speak for yourself. What are you afraid of, whom are you trying to screen? Nice sort of husband you have, I must say – sent you to prison. What will you do about your child? Send him to an institution? You were busy with books and science, conclusions and deductions, and here he was going about restaurants with pretty girls! What do you say to that?' He paused, watching the effect.

There was none. I was wondering what new trick he would try on me this time.

'Do you know who Lidochka is?'

'My former domestic help.'

'Ha, ha! That's a funny coincidence! No, no, she is not a domestic help at all, but a very pretty girl. Though perhaps your maid too was pretty, eh? So you don't know who she is?'

'No.'

'That's a pity. That husband of yours knows her very well.'

'That's his affair.'

'How do you mean, his affair? He squanders your money with a pretty lady and you don't care?'

'Whether he squandered it or not, it was his money. I had my own earnings and spent my money as I liked.'

'Oh, stop that intellectual nonsense! Why do you give yourself airs? Your husband drank and squandered money on women, and you? Ha-ha-ha! Spent your time reading books, eh? You'd have done better looking after your husband – you wouldn't have been here then. Well, what do you say, then?'

He said much more on the subject trying on me one of the most vulgar catches that seldom succeeds with even the worst type of women, because the motive behind it is too obvious. I was quite interested to discover one more of his tricks, especially meant for women. Judging by detective novels which I came across in prison it was an old-fashioned trick, but I doubt if in the old days it was applied to cultured people. Now OGPU officials tried it on virtuous elderly ladies who had got over their romantic feelings a good twenty years before and listened with surprise to coarse insinuations made by the representatives of political power in the State.

But even if this trick did not attain its primary object of rousing jealousy and making a woman speak against her husband, it was one more way of insulting her dignity. It was not for nothing that the noseless face of the former prostitute in the red kerchief gave me such a shock. There was something nasty in the whole atmosphere of the prison, as there is bound to be wherever man is given unlimited power over his fellow creatures.

At every fresh interview the examining officer did his best to make me sink lower and lower: to frighten and humiliate me so that I should lose all sense of personal dignity and become a spiritless, miserable wreck, ready to do anything if only I were allowed to live.

.

.

CHAPTER XVII

THE CHARGE

AFTER seven such interviews in succession, I felt more bewildered than ever. The examining officer threatened me with death, talked humiliating nonsense, but he never told me what the charge against me was. Under those circumstances I was just as likely to be shot as to be set free. The most sensible thing for me would have been to admit that the whole of the OGPU procedure is absolutely arbitrary, but ideas of justice and of rational motives inspiring the activity of State institutions had too firm a hold on my mind. And so I tried to discover the general trend of the OGPU policy by watching the treatment of other prisoners, whom I mentally divided into various categories. It was not easy for me to make observations because I was supposed to be in solitary confinement. But as the prison was overcrowded, I either had to share somebody else's cell, or other women were put into mine. They brought a supply of news and information which we eked out by what we could see through the prison window when prisoners kept in common cells were taken to walk in the yard.

The biggest category was that of 'wives', which included also sisters, nieces, mothers and sometimes even grandmothers. Several families were represented by three generations and many by two. Imprisonment of relatives was called 'bringing social pressure' to bear upon the head of the family; in themselves they were of no account. The wives were sometimes cross-examined, but other relatives were simply kept in prison. This was done to harass the head of the family and also to deprive him of any outside help. When sentence was passed on him, his wife generally received a sentence one degree lighter than he – even though she had nothing to do with his case. If the husband was sentenced to ten years penal servitude, she was sentenced to five; if he got five years, she got three. Other relatives were as a rule banished to distant parts for five or three years.

The second category included women who had been abroad since the Revolution, though they had gone with full permission of the Government. Most of them were being punished for going abroad in 1925-6, when, thanks to NEP the rouble stood high and foreign passports were issued comparatively easily, especially if one left good hostages behind. Many were imprisoned for having in the past unsuccessfully applied for a foreign passport. Others were imprisoned for succumbing to the temptation of buying from private dealers foreign stockings, scent or powder (these goods were often sold by OGPU agents). They were all of them accused of 'espionage' (article 58, 6 of the Soviet Code). At best they were sentenced to exile to remote parts of the country – the Urals or Siberia – but generally to five or ten years penal servitude in Solovki or other concentration camps. Those to whom friends or relatives abroad sent money, letters or parcels also came under the charge of espionage, though they received it all through perfectly legal channels.

Women belonging to this group were hardly ever released.

The third category, which also had no hope of release, included those who suffered for their religion – nuns from the convents that had been closed, pious women who helped churches or priests, wives and daughters of the clergy. Most of them regarded their imprisonment as a punishment from God or as part of the persecution of the faithful foretold in the Revelation. The examining officer took little interest in them and practically all of them were sent to penal camps for five or ten years. Struggle against religion forms part of the Government programme; it has never ceased, and now that most of the important people are dead or in exile, the OGPU has to be content with 'small fry'.

Common criminals were in a different position. There were comparatively few of them, only some ten per cent. Dressed in skirts that did not reach to the knee, dishevelled, with big busts and loud voices, they swore at the wardresses, gibed at everyone, continually quarrelled among themselves and sometimes fought, clutching desperately at each other's hair and doing their best to scratch each other's faces. They had the greatest contempt for us, stole our things and played us nasty tricks not so much out of malice as because they thought us stupid and helpless. They jeered at us for being no good at telling lies, for being in prison 'for nothing' and especially for our politeness. In many ways they were probably more sensible than we, because they fought for their rights and secured every advantage they could; but it was very trying to live with them, especially when in common cells a hundred prisoners were crowded into a room meant for twenty.

I remember thinking what a bitter mockery it was for the Soviet newspapers to attack Polish prisons where, they said, political prisoners were treated like common criminals. The OGPU's method was much simpler: they regarded us all as common criminals and therefore did not bother to give us any advantages over thieves and prostitutes. Indeed, those who were guilty of some real offence received the lightest punishments: three or five years of concentration camps, where their sentence was speedily reduced. Many of them ran away, certain that they would find refuge in the big towns until they were caught at some fresh theft. Used to defying social order they felt thoroughly at home in prison: they laughed at the OGPU and were so enterprising that once they managed to steal a suit-case from the prison office. The man in charge of the office had to spend a month in his own prison as a punishment for his negligence.

The only political prisoners who had individual charges brought against them were Mensheviks, Trotskyists and former Social-Revolutionaries; sometimes respectable Party workers of the period of 1905, whose names were entered in the *History of the Party.* Those of them who had been in the Tsarist prisons amused us very much by their indignation at the present penal system. They occasionally indulged in fine speeches about 'freedom', 'rights of the individual', 'humaneness' and other things which sounded more naïve than any fairy tale. The OGPU regarded them as 'politicals', i.e., gave them a piece of meat in their soup, but treated them sternly; for the most part they were sent to Moscow where some of them had already been in the 'Polit-Isolator'*. From there they were transferred to a special concentration camp in the Northern Urals.

The charges against the first three categories of women prisoners – the 'wives', those who had been abroad and religious women – were absurdly out of keeping with the actual reason for their arrest. Thus, purchasing silk stockings was described as 'espionage on behalf of foreign capitalists'; belonging to an aristocratic family figured as 'monarchist propaganda'; being related to an engineer meant 'helping and abetting the wreckers' activities'; receiving letters from relatives abroad or writing to them was classed as 'furthering foreign intervention' and so on. The sentences were almost invariably five or ten – seldom three – years of penal servitude in the concentration camps. 'Free exile' to East Siberia, Northern or Southern Urals and Viatka often proved to be even worse than the camps, because it was impossible to find work in out-of-the-way villages, and the exiles were given neither money nor rations. Solitude in those wilds was to some people more terrible than the crowded camps.

Apparently, the same fate awaited me, and it was only a question of the number of years. Five or ten years was no joke, especially when they might be my last years. But other women were worse off than I, for they went into exile leaving several children behind. My fellow prisoners kept telling me that there was still hope, for I had not yet received my 'accusation'. It was supposed to be handed to the prisoners not later

* A special prison in the Lubianka for erring Communists, social-revolutionaries and anarchists.

than a fortnight after the arrest, but was always delayed, generally for two or three months, or more.

I received mine very soon. Three weeks after my arrest I was taken again to the examining officer who interviewed me in the first instance. He had just come into the room and was unlocking his case, pulling out of it bundles of pinkish papers. These were the 'accusations' which, to save time, were prepared wholesale. He silently handed me one of them. It was marked by a number exceeding a thousand, though we were still in the third month of the year; it had written on it that I was accused of 'furthering economic counter-revolution'.

'What is required of me?' I asked, understanding that there was no point in speaking about the accusation, which I simply did not understand; neither of the OGPU officers who examined me ever asked me a single question relating to it.

'Sign that you have been informed of the charge against you.'

I signed as firmly and clearly as I could.

'Go back to your cell.'

I did as I was told.

I was not called up for any more interviews. Everything seemed to have been settled. No explanations were required; no defence was possible. I had now to wait for the verdict, which would no doubt be as absurd as the charge.

I could not have explained what 'economic counter-revolution' meant, to say nothing of my 'furthering' it; history, literature and art were the subjects at which I had worked all my life. But charges against other prisoners were just as senseless, so that I was no exception.

CHAPTER XVIII

'Churches and prisons we'll
pull to the ground'

A Soviet song.

AFTER presenting me with the accusation the OGPU
forgot my existence for four and a half months.

In Tsarist prisons preliminary inquiry did not take
long and, once the sentence was passed, the prisoner
knew that every day brought him nearer freedom. In
U.S.S.R. preliminary 'inquiry' lasts five or six months
and sometimes more than a year. During the most
reactionary periods of Tsardom political prisoners were
never to be reckoned by hundreds; they all belonged
either to revolutionary parties or to more or less active
political groups. In U.S.S.R. the total number of
prisoners and convicts in penal camps exceeds a million,
and with the rarest exceptions, none of them belong to
any political organisation. Thousands of peasants are
exiled without any trial or inquiry; educated men –
experts and their families – are imprisoned for months
and months during the fictitious 'inquiry' into their
case. Of late years, when the Bolsheviks have attacked
the intellectuals with special ferocity, such numbers of

125

them were imprisoned that there was not a family left
some member of which was not in prison or exile.

When the charge had been presented to me and I
had lost all hope of release, prison life began to get hold
of me more and more. It was not life but a special
regime aimed at destroying one's will, capacity for
work, feeling of personal dignity and sense of duty.
One's existence was confined to a cell with stone walls
and a low vaulted ceiling; it was six feet long and there
was a distance of two feet between the iron bedsteads
with hard and dirty straw mattresses. An iron stool
and a small table, the heating pipe, a wash basin and
an open lavatory seat completed the furnishing

The window – our only joy – was placed near the
ceiling and covered with a close iron grating. In winter
the glass was covered with a thick layer of ice. The
pane that opened had a sheet of iron over it, with
small holes cut in the iron. What came through it was
not fresh air, but heavy steam from the kitchen and a
smell of stale cabbage soup.

The iron door was awe inspiring: it seemed unthinkable that it would ever open to let us out, but at night
we were led through it to be cross-examined, or might
be led to be shot. When at nine in the evening the
night wardress locked all doors turning the key three
times, saying 'Sleep! Sleep! Sleep!' and turned out the
lights we heard heavy, menacing footsteps coming
from the depths of the prison – the soldier on duty was
coming for a victim. Everyone sat up and listened
breathless with agitation.

He was on the stairs . . . turning the corner . . . his
boot caught at the step and he stumbled . . . he was just
coming . . . no – he went past! And sometimes he did

not go past but standing at the door spelt out to himself the name written on his list.

There was a click of the switch, a naked light right in one's eyes, the shutter in the door rattled, and a coarse face with a blank expression appeared in it.

'What's your name? You are wanted!'

Interviews with the examining officer might mean life or death to the prisoners, and to the officers they often were a means of relaxation. Cultured, honourable women who had not done any wrong, were questioned for hours by the shameless, demoralised agents of the OGPU, who practised on us every kind of insult and mockery. They felt more free at night, and the doors of our cells opened for us to be led to this moral torture.

Both day and night prisoners were watched through the 'peep-hole' – an oval opening in the door, glazed and covered over with a metal shield; it was used two or three times an hour. In the daytime this was irritating, especially when the spying was done not by wardresses but by warders, all of them, as though of design, coarse and impudent men; but at night it was perfect torture. Along all the floors, at the door of every cell the switch clicked twice; the sound grew louder and louder till it reached one's door; a bright light cut one's eyes, the shield of the peep-hole was closed again, the light went out and the clicking continued further off. No sooner had one dozed off than the whole thing began over again, and so it went on all night because the checking was done every twenty minutes and lasted a good ten minutes each time. Everyone suffered from it; some covered their heads with the blanket, which was forbidden and caused altercation with the warders, others tied up their eyes and ears with a kerchief so as to be less disturbed by the light and the noise. It may not have been intended to make us suffer, but it was very bad for the nerves not to have a single peaceful night for months.

And so days, weeks and months passed in that dirty hole between the terrible iron door and the grated window.

Seven o'clock in the morning – getting up time. It is horrible to have to get up when one has no work, no occupation but only fourteen empty hours to live through. A worn brush is thrust in at the door to sweep the floor with; then a piece of black bread is brought – one pound per day, and instead of tea, lukewarm water, which is carried about from cell to cell in huge kettles and poured out into metal mugs. Within half an hour all the day's work is finished. A special warder takes two prisoners out of the solitary confinement cells for a walk. The walk is supposed to last fifteen minutes but he takes off two minutes for the journey along the corridors and cuts it short by another three because he is in a hurry to finish and go off to his dinner.

The walk is in the prison yard which is thirty feet wide and sixty feet long; prison buildings, five-stories high, surround it on all sides so that there is hardly any sun there and only a small piece of the sky is visible. The court is asphalt and not a bit of earth shows anywhere. In winter it is covered with dirty snow, completely trampled down.

When I was in prison I happened to see on the wrapper of some Soviet magazine a photograph of a prison-yard in Spain; under it was a grandiloquent inscription about bourgeois terrorism. It was a big yard with shady trees growing around it, and the prisoners – no doubt common criminals – were walking along a path strewn with sand. We kept that picture for weeks and gazed at it dreamily after our walks.

But anyway, a walk was a joy: the door was opened, we were let out of the hateful cell, we saw our neighbours and could exchange a look of sympathy. In the courtyard, other prisoners looked at us from the windows of the common cells – at the risk of being deprived of a walk themselves as punishment; we, too, sometimes saw interesting sights. Two of the women had babies born in prison and they carried them in their arms when walking in the yard. In the spring, when huge parties of prisoners were being sent to parts of Northern Russia that could not be reached in winter, children from outside appeared in prison. The first time that we heard a child's voice in the yard we could hardly believe our ears.

'Is it a boy?' we tried to decide by the sound.

'It is!'

Both my fellow prisoner and I had sons left at home, and it gave us an extraordinary thrill of joy to hear a child's voice, though it was horrible to think of a child being in prison. My neighbour jumped on to the bed so as to peep out of the window.

'It's a boy, a little peasant boy; he's walking with his mother. He bumps into her for fun and then runs away. . . .'

'Let me have a look!' I begged. 'Yes, it is a boy! About six, I should think. Funny little thing! He has a huge cap on, his father's probably, and his boots are all torn and patched.'

We eagerly watched him all the time he was in the courtyard. After half an hour's walk which was allowed to those kept in the common cell, he went back to it with his mother.

'What does it mean?' we asked each other in surprise.

'I suppose they first exiled the father and then arrested the mother, and she had to take the child with her to prison.'

'But it's absurd – a child in prison!'

'He won't be any better off in the penal camps, you know.'

I said nothing.

I have no words to tell how I yearned for that child, how sweet it was to hear his voice and footsteps in the yard. He spent about three weeks in prison, and then another boy appeared in his place. The second was a quiet, clean little boy in a neat sailor suit. During the first few days he was afraid of the warder and clung to his mother, but soon a little girl appeared to keep him company. She was about eight, older than he was and more bold: they rushed about the yard, chasing each other, and afterwards sat locked up all day in the stuffy and crowded cell, waiting to be sent to the penal camp.

It was a special favour that the 'criminal' mothers – 'kulaks' and 'rotten bourgeois' – were allowed to have their children in prison instead of sending them to an institution for homeless children, where the examining officer threatened to send my son. I do not know how that favour was obtained; perhaps Comrade Krupskaya herself persuaded the OGPU not to part the children from their mothers, but anyway in the spring of 1931 I saw those children in prison – and I honestly could not say whether I envied their mothers or not.

The appearance of children in prison was an exciting event, and the minutes of watching them passed quickly, but afterwards hours again seemed like years. From seven in the morning till two o'clock when dinner was brought there was time enough to get in a good working day, but for us there was only the misery of idleness and pacing up and down the cell like caged beasts.

For dinner huge cauldrons of smelly, over-cooked cabbage soup were brought. It was poured out into aluminium cups, very much like dogs' basins, and thrust into the opening in the door. Sometimes one found in it a piece of stringy meat, the size of a cubic centimetre. 'Politicals', i.e., Communists had meat soup of better quality. For second course all had millet porridge so over-cooked that it was one sticky, dough-like mass.

The food was hideous; not hunger but the feeling that one must eat to live made one swallow some of it. After dinner we were allowed to lie down for two hours. Though sleep was full of sinister dreams and fears, it was better than the emptiness of the waking hours.

At four o'clock came the call 'get up!'

But the evening was easier to bear: daytime, in which everyone had been used to work, was gone. We talked and recalled the past which seemed long and rich and vivid. All our memories acquired a new value, as before death. But the thought of death had lost its terrors when life was confined to an empty existence in a stone cage. The thought of exile was more alarming.

Some former occupant of the cell had written on the wall a crude poem that had a very real meaning for us:

> And may be in exile
> In a barrack of planks
> Where icy wind
> Drives the snow through the cracks,
> We'll look back on the cell
> And the bedstead of iron
> And the door that shuts so well.

Was it possible that we could sink so low as to regret the prison? We were certainly kept alive and fed, and had no need to work. Our sole occupation was to kill time, as though life were long enough for that!

·

CHAPTER XIX

THE OGPU did not like people to die in prison and tried to prevent it – death was the speciality of the penal camps. It only sought to weaken us morally and physically so that we should have no power of resistance left. In the Press, it is true, the Bolsheviks represented their regime in very different colours; Ramzin, Fedotov and others who figured at the public trial had to declare that their health improved in prison where they had 'constant medical attendance'. I do not question their statement. They had leading parts to play and before they appeared on the stage they must have been taken care of. But people like myself were not wanted for publicity purposes and so there was no occasion to look after us; though for the sake of appearances there was a medical staff in prison. Indeed, some of the staff were always on the spot in case of attempted suicide, which the OGPU tried to prevent. Besides, it was the chief doctor's special duty to certify that the prisoners who had been shot were really dead.

After my interviews with the 'lively' examining officer when I had to strain every nerve to keep my self-control, my health gave out: I developed red patches on my skin that itched, turned wet and wrinkled. It looked rather awful. My neighbour who was fond of repeating a wise saying that 'One's own dirt is better than other people's infection', decided that I must have caught something dreadful trying to clean the filthy straw mattress or washing myself in the so-called bath. The bathroom where we were taken once a fortnight certainly was a frightening place. It was an almost square cell without windows or any ventilation. By the back wall stood a huge shapeless copper bath dating back to the times of Alexander II. Its edges were broken and crumpled and it was slimy and slippery inside. It would never occur to anyone to fill it with water and use it as a proper bath, but one had to step into it because the taps were inside and there was a douche over it. The general impression of primeval filth was made worse by the look of the walls: the paint had cracked with the heat and was coming off in bits; the ceiling was almost as black as the asphalt floor. The concentrated stench of the place took one's breath away. But we had to wash somehow and there was nowhere else to do it.

I had to ask for a doctor, if only to make sure that I would not infect my neighbour. A doctor's assistant appeared. She dashed into the cell accompanied by the wardress and before I had had time to say a word she declared 'Slight infection, don't wash, I'll send you an ointment', and dashed out again. She carried out in all conscience the rule that members of the medical staff must not talk to the prisoners. A little later the wardress shoved through the slot in the door a packet with some ointment. My neighbour sniffed it: 'It is exactly the same that she sent me when I had earache.' Afterwards my other neighbours received that same ointment for abscesses, hæmorroids and many other complaints.

When I was released from prison and went to a real doctor, he was much surprised at the treatment prescribed to me. My trouble, it appears, was nervous eczema which ought to be washed and not anointed.

'But surely there was a doctor in prison?' he asked me.

'Yes, but only his assistant could call him in. She could do so if she felt that she was not competent to deal with the case. Considering the hurry she was in, that was not likely to happen often.'

As a matter of fact, I did see the prison doctor on two occasions. My neighbour had an attack of appendicitis. The doctor came, prodded her in the spot where the appendix is supposed to be and asked:

'Here?'

'Yes. Doctor, I cannot . . .' But before she had finished the sentence, the doctor turned round and was gone. The cell door banged and we were left staring at each other in astonishment.

Another neighbour I had, an elderly woman, had a violent attack of angina. That happened during cross-examination and as examining officers do not like prisoners to die before their case is concluded, the doctor was sent into the cell almost as soon as she had been carried into it. He felt her pulse and walked out without saying or doing anything. Evidently there was no immediate danger of death. The wardress and I spent the whole night nursing her as she kept gasping for breath and losing consciousness, but we did not send for the doctor any more.

I have been told that when, in the common cell, this doctor was called to a patient who had been delirious for two days, he declared:

'Remember, I come only to the dead and the paralysed. Don't disturb me for nothing.'

Though perhaps it would have been more absurd for doctors to try and cure those whom the OGPU had doomed to death or to Solovki.

That summer, however, when scurvy assumed proportions that seemed alarming even to the OGPU, the prison authorities displayed unexpected solicitude.

At an unusual time of the day we heard keys rattling and doors banging everywhere. Our door also flew open. A doctor came in, an elderly man getting on to sixty, obviously of the old school; he wore a white overall but had a cigarette in his mouth. Without taking it out he commanded:

'Eye!' and roughly turned up my eyelid.

'Teeth!' he shoved his finger in my mouth and rubbed my gums.

'Leg!' he felt my knee.

Without washing his hands he did the same thing to my neighbour – this time a common criminal suffering from venereal disease – and sending a whiff of smoke into her nose, went out. His visit may have lasted a minute; then the door next to us banged and he went into the next cell. The quickness of the examination, to say nothing of the simplified hygienic methods, certainly beat all records.

But even if he did infect someone the good result of his visit was that on the next 'parcel day' we received what had so far been strictly forbidden: raw carrots, radishes, onions, garlic and fresh cucumbers. Prisoners we had not seen before were taken to walk in the courtyard. What a sight they were! One, quite young, could hardly move and dragged one leg painfully.

Another, almost a child, dressed in a girl's blouse with a sailor collar, just managed to walk as far as the warder's stool; she sank on to it, looked at the sky and wept. A third, an elderly woman whose fine, severe face reminded one of an old ikon, was carried out on her bed – she was not able to walk. As she was carried back to her cell she gave one long look at the sky and made the sign of the cross.

Forgetful of all precautions we hung on the window, trembling with excitement: these women came from the 'dead' cells, whose inmates had never before been let out into the fresh air. One of them happened to be in the yard while I was there; she could scarcely move, and I was able to overtake her several times so as to express my sympathy, by a look at any rate. She understood me and whispered as I walked past:

'Six months without fresh air, without books or papers.'

Six months, one hundred and eighty days in which she heard nothing except the examining officer's insults and jeers – and we had been complaining because we were given only four books in ten days, one of them a 'political' book, i.e., some old collection of Communistic speeches or of polemics between Deborin and Axelrod, accusing each other of being idiots and of interpreting Hegel's dialectic in a non-Marxist way.

Plehanov in his article about the Decembrists, says that we must not blame Pestel for his penitent letter to Nicolas I because he had had five months of solitary confinement. But, though it was one of the darkest periods of Tsardom, Pestel, who had raised an armed rebellion, was allowed a Bible, paper and ink; the Socialistic Government of 'the freest country in the world' condemned women whose guilt had not yet been established by the OGPU, to an existence that was little better than a living death. If Pestel lost courage, what was to be expected of these women? Some of them went mad, others committed suicide, but the rest remained true to themselves and went into exile with the same quiet fortitude.

·

CHAPTER XX

TEARS

'Loud speaking, singing and tears are forbidden.'

One of the prison rules.

I N their anxiety to reduce our inner life to nothing, the OGPU went so far as to forbid us to cry, although in our state of nervous exhaustion many found it impossible to refrain from tears. Of course one could cry quietly, closing the eyes or pretending a headache, but as soon as the wardress noticed it through the peephole, the slot in the door went up and there followed rude remonstrances that there was nothing to cry for, that we mustn't, that it was forbidden.

When old wardresses shouted in their rough but simple-hearted way, 'What's the good of blubbering, stop it, now!' it did not sound half so offensive as the remarks of the young Communists with painted lips and plucked eyebrows, who had just been promoted to the rank of wardresses. They said with a snort of contempt, 'For shame! You should have more self-respect. Stop, or I'll tell the chief warder!'

But some of the prisoners were too ill and nervous to control themselves, and then there was trouble.

At dusk, when darkness gathered in the cells, but for

the sake of economy no lights were lit, one felt particularly miserable. Nothing could be more depressing than that cold sepulchral darkness; the cell seemed like the grave. Everyone felt wretched during that last half-hour before the lights were turned on. I remember I said once to the old wardress:

'If ever I hang myself, it will be at dusk.'

'Oh, don't say such things!' she said in genuine alarm. 'I should be pleased to turn the light on, but it's not allowed,' she added apologetically. 'We have to save on lighting. As it is, I light up five minutes earlier than I ought. If only Number Two doesn't begin to cry! That will be more trouble than it is worth.'

In prison we were known by our numbers, not by names. We never saw Number Two, because she was not let out for walks, but we knew her voice very well – she could not endure the dusk and often wept.

She wept quietly, though sometimes a sob escaped her, and if she was left in peace she gradually calmed down. But prison discipline demanded that measures should be taken at once, and then there was a scene. It began with the wardress's running up and down the iron stairs, opening the slot in her door and speaking to her in a menacing voice, which was answered by bitter sobs. Then the chief warder's boots were heard thundering up the stairs, and he roared threateningly:

'I'll put you in a punishment cell!'

She cried more bitterly, like a child who cannot stop. In the dead stillness disturbed only by the rattle of keys and the steps of the warders, the sound of this unfortunate woman weeping in her solitary cell, made us feel as though she were lamenting over all of us, buried alive in the prison.

The chief warder went to fetch two heavy-footed assistants.

'To the punishment cell!'

The woman's weeping became a wail; the key rattled, the door opened with a sinister noise and the place rang with heartrending screams:

'Leave me, let me be! There are rats there! I'm afraid of them! Don't take me there!'

They dragged her by force, pulling her along the floor, while she struggled and screamed, wild with despair, choking with tears and the horror of the rat-infested punishment cell. All the five stories of the prison resounded with her cries, and then came a stillness that was even more terrible. No one ever heard how she came back to her cell. Intimidated by the punishment, she would sometimes control herself for a week or ten days, but sometimes the fits of weeping recurred almost every day and with the same results.

One evening when I was led back to my cell after a cross-examination I saw a dreadful scene: in the narrow corridor on the ground floor this woman, worn out by sobbing and struggling, was being pushed into the door of the punishment cell. The broad back of one of the warders shut her off from my view, and I only saw her head, with lovely fair hair that fell in disorder on her deadly pale, tear-stained face. She was groaning but still trying to resist, though her arms were held by two burly men.

'A rat!' she screamed, panic-stricken, and the heavy iron door shut her in.

There were huge rats in the prison. At one time the authorities tried to exterminate them and put down poison; the rats came out of their holes to die in the courtyard, and their hideous reddish corpses with bare tails could be seen by the walls, on the half-basement window-sills and in the middle of the yard.

It may be very foolish and feminine, but the sight of a dead rat spoiled all the pleasure of the walk in the courtyard. I dread to think what it must have been like in the punishment cell, the ceiling of which was said to be so low that one could not stand up, and where the warders could put out the light, leaving their victim in darkness alone with the rats.

Another prisoner who was constantly punished for weeping was probably half-insane. She often began by singing, which was strictly forbidden. She had a beautiful voice and had obviously been trained for operatic singing, but her style was very peculiar: she sang the most cheerful songs to funereal tunes, and sad ones – such as Lisa's aria in the *Queen of Spades* – like a chansonette. She did it admirably, and her voice grew louder and louder; the wardress interposed and threatened her, then she cried and sobbed hysterically. Sometimes she began by crying, but she did it in her own way: she cooed in a sad little voice like a turtle dove, then the sound grew stronger, and she wailed in a sing-song voice louder and louder, but always very musically.

Then we heard the wardress's remonstrances and the chief warder's threats, which she answered by wild screaming and cursing. But evidently she was regarded as insane, because instead of locking her in the punishment cell they put her in a strait waistcoat and tied her to her bed. Worn out by crying and struggling, she gradually subsided.

The prison authorities hated her, probably because they could not deal with her in their own way; they kept her in one of the darkest and dampest cells on the ground floor, and did not allow her out for walks; only once in the summer she was taken out into the courtyard. She proved to be a young woman, tall and well-made, with charming manners; she stepped along the yard as though it were a ballroom, spoke pleasantly to the warder in charge of her, and burst into song as soon as she was brought back to her cell. She was not let out any more.

It was a mystery what the OGPU wanted with this poor mad woman, whom they kept for nearly a year in prison; they do not hesitate to fake evidence, and could have done so in her case instead of driving her to hopeless insanity. We were, of course, unable to do or say anything; we did not even know her name, and could never discover what was finally done to her.

The third woman who attracted attention by her weeping was the common criminal who at one time shared my cell. With her, tears were a means of obtaining favours from prison authorities. It generally happened when she was short of cigarettes. Longing for tobacco she wandered aimlessly about the cell, killed flies, scratched the paint on the walls, and then announced to me:

'I am going to set up a concert and get some cigarettes.' She sat down on her bed and began rocking herself to and fro, wailing piteously:

'My poor, poor mother! What are they doing to me! Mother, mother! Why did you bring me into the world! Poor, unhappy me!'

Upset by her own words, she began shedding real

tears, entering into her part more and more thoroughly.

'I shall die, I shall die, never see you again!'

She put in a line from a popular song and broke into loud sobs.

The wardress's remonstrations were of no avail, because only the chief warder could get cigarettes from the OGPU buffet. When he appeared and sternly asked: 'What is it now? What do you want, citizen?' she calmed down, gave him a sad, appealing look – which suited her young and pretty face very well – and whispered, 'A cigarette!'

Surprised by such an easy solution of the trouble, he grinned, and pulling out a smart cigarette-case adorned with monograms, provided her with cigarettes.

'Don't you receive any parcels?' he asked sympathetically.

'Yes, but I never have enough,' she complained. 'It's so dull here. Send to buy me some more, dear!'

She begged a rouble of me on the spot and made the chief warder promise that he would have some cigarettes bought for her – an unheard of concession, which only she knew how to obtain.

.

CHAPTER XXI

PIGEONS

OUR only joy in prison were the pigeons. In the spring there were many of them. With a soft rustle of wings they flew over the stone walls of the prison, alighting on the dirty melting snow of the yard, where everyone during the walk tried to leave for them some bread crumbs or lumps of porridge. Cooing they walked about on the roof, and we heard their feet pattering on the iron window-sills of the prison windows.

On Easter Day someone managed to leave in the corner of the yard an egg with 'Christ is Risen' written on it; the egg was painted, in prison-fashion, with indelible pencil and coloured threads, probably pulled out of a dress. An Easter egg would not have been allowed in a parcel from home. Pigeons crowded round it, and pecked at it busily, scattering bits of coloured shell. This is how people in Russia greet their dead on Easter Day – by leaving coloured eggs on the graves for birds to peck at.

How strange that after two thousand years mankind was still the same – Judases and Pilates, executions, martyrdom!

On Easter Monday there was torrential rain and wild wind. Windows in the OGPU agents' flats, above the common cells, flew open and bits of paper fluttered about. The following morning we found in the yard a blue flower made of fine shavings – a Soviet invention, since paper and rags are much too dear. It looked lovely, but no one dared to take it; we were not allowed to pick up even pigeons' feathers.

In a semi-basement window that we had to pass on the way to the yard lay some freshly-sawn logs that had a delicious smell of the forest. It gave one the illusion of being really out in the open, but the rude shout, 'Go on, what are you stopping for!' brought one back to the sour stench of the prison.

These were chance incidents, but the pigeons came continually, pecked the bread crumbs on the window-sill, and peeped into the cell, stretching their necks and holding their heads on one side as though surprised by what they saw.

Feeding the pigeons was strictly forbidden; both the wardresses inside the prison and the warders outside, who could see on whose windows the pigeons settled, persecuted us for it. But it was very hard to part with our only visitors!

Not to be caught at these forbidden trysts, I fed my pigeons at a quiet secret hour. When lights were put out for the night I stealthily got up from my bed, stole up to the window and, opening the ventilation pane, strewed bread crumbs on the window-sill. At daybreak when, after a disturbed night, everyone dozed off at last – the wardresses, the sentry in the yard, and even the most nervous and restless of the prisoners, pigeons cheerfully flew to my window. They pecked greedily, fighting and pushing each other, cooing contentedly when there was enough and peeping at the window with a request for more.

I listened to them through my sleep, sorry that the hour for getting up was drawing near and another senseless day would soon begin. The sound of their cooing that came into the cell, together with a whiff of fresh morning air not poisoned as yet by the kitchen fumes made one think of freedom. Summer, sunshine on the free blue sea, a far-off, cloudless sky. My little boy is swimming and diving in shallow water like a white puppy, and sharp-winged gulls are flying over him. He screams with joy and laughs, spitting out the salty water. Was he laughing now, left alone among strangers?

'Dear, friendly birds, it's time you flew away! You little care that the sentry is waking up, that the wardress begins her walk down the corridors, but I'll get into trouble.'

I was sorry to drive them away and hear no more of their cooing. I never fed them in the daytime, though they came to the window and scolded me in angry, loud voices.

But soon the OGPU destroyed our harmless, charming friends. Orders were issued that they were all to be caught and killed. A trap was put in the yard and the tame, friendly birds were almost all caught within a few days. A pigeon and two doves still came to my window, but I did not feed them any more in spite of all their grumbling and complaints. I wanted them to lose the habit of coming and fly away to safety. But no! Soon I found the pigeon lying dead in the trap; the doves disappeared. The courtyard grew still and empty; only the prisoners dejectedly paced to and fro on the black asphalt.

．

CHAPTER XXII

THE LAST INTERVIEW WITH THE OGPU

SUMMER passed: June, July. We were perishing with the heat and the stuffiness. The thick stone walls exuded moisture that had been accumulating for years and years. The cells were hot and damp, like a bad cellar. Though we had no exercise and scarcely moved at all, we were bathed in perspiration day and night. All were getting thinner and paler than in winter, while the wardresses looked jolly and sunburnt.

It was nearly five months since my arrest; four months since the accusation was shown to me, and almost ten since my husband was taken. I knew nothing of what was happening outside the prison, and could not understand when our 'case' would end.

'You must wait,' the old wardresses said. They had grown used to me and were sympathetic. 'It's always like that with us: if they don't let you out at the end of two months, you must wait five. And it's a good sign that they don't call you up to be questioned.'

Almost all the women in solitary confinement had been sentenced to five or ten years of penal camps. They were waiting for the sentence to be confirmed by the Moscow OGPU, which settled their fate without having ever heard their own evidence. A dull indifference descended upon them during those last days before exile into the cold and hunger of the penal camps. The woman whose cell I shared on my first night in prison had been sentenced to death, but the sentence was commuted to ten years penal servitude at Solovki. For me, too, the days dragged on dully and aimlessly.

Suddenly I was called before the examining officer. That meant the end. What was it?

It is impossible to describe what I felt as I went to hear my verdict. A blind fury of indignation was welling up within me. To think that I should have to submit in silence to an absurd sentence passed on me and my husband and my child by the dullards of the OGPU!

It all seemed like a bad dream: the examining officer's study, the branch outside his window, though this time its leaves were dusty and withered. The same horrid, hysterical man.

'Take a seat.'

He looked me up and down.

'You are looking very well.'

'And so are you.'

'Yes, you know I have been away on leave. I have kept you waiting. Were you bored?'

'It's not particularly cheerful here.'

A wry smile.

'Quite so, quite so.' He opened his cigarette-case: 'And your dear husband has been sent to penal servitude. Yes! We don't want wreckers. Certainly not!' he shouted.

So that was the end. They have sent him away.

'Where to?' I asked, speaking with difficulty.

'I don't know. To the north, I believe, to the penal camps. Let him knock about for two or three years there and learn to work, instead of wrecking. It will do him good.'

'When was he sent?' I asked calmly, though I felt sick and dizzy.

'I don't know. How should I know? It was not my case,' he said carelessly, watching me with interest. 'Well, what about you? Where shall we send you? We thought of Solovki. What do you say to that?'

He kept his eyes on me, waiting to see the effect. I said nothing.

'Yes, yes. We thought of Solovki. It's a fine place. The sea, forest all round.'

He went on chattering. I did not hear and could not force myself to listen or to think of my own fate. They have sent my husband away. He doesn't tell me where nor when. I haven't been allowed to see him, they didn't let us say good-bye.

'We thought of Solovki, but we took pity on you. You have a son, you know. We've been keeping an eye on him. He is not a bad boy, but we don't want homeless children. So you'll have to work for the present, yes, to work.'

'Where?'

'How do you mean, where? At your old job. You are of no interest to us now. What did you think? They showed you some sort of charge against you, didn't they? That's nonsense! We just write out those charges when necessary. You can forget about that. I repeat, we are no longer interested in you and you are no use to us. It's true. I was very much annoyed with you and seriously wanted to send you to Solovki. I have no patience with the way one has to wring out every word from you. It's beyond everything! However, we've decided to let you off and you may go. But I don't advise you to return to us, I certainly don't. Next time we should have a different sort of talk. I don't believe you understand what I am saying – I tell you, we are letting you go. I am just going to sign the order. It has to go to the office, and to-night, or to-morrow morning, as soon as the formalities are finished, you may go home! I have kept you here a bit too long, but never mind, you'll have plenty of time to get over it. Take care you don't fall into our hands again! We won't stand on ceremony with you then.'

I sat there wondering how much longer he would go on. Was he expecting me to thank him for having sent my husband to penal servitude, kept me in prison, and spoiled the boy's life?

'Go and wait.'

At last! I came out feeling quite broken and could hardly crawl back to my cell. They did not come to release me that evening. I did not mind. I felt that by myself I could master my sorrow better; I dreaded returning to the home which my husband would never see again.

I did not sleep all night – the same hopeless thoughts haunted me. One good thing about prison is that it makes everything stand still; it frightens one to return to the wreckage of the life outside.

Morning came. I was taken for my walk. Other prisoners looked at me in surprise – I looked so ill. I cannot think what I had been hoping for, but the future seemed to me terrible.

'What has happened?' whispered the women from the cell next to mine, overtaking me.

'My husband has been sent to a penal camp. When, where – I don't know.'

'I am going to be released,' I added as I met them on the second round.

They were delighted. It was a joy for all to hear that someone was released.

The day dragged on. There had never been a longer day.

Another sleepless night. I kept thinking that I would not have time to see my husband before he died in the penal camp. What he must have felt going there and leaving me in prison!

Another morning. My neighbour, the pretty girl from the streets, laughed at me.

'Your eyes have sunk in, you look older by ten years. The examining officer must have given it you for your nice goings-on if you look such a sight.'

I said nothing. I had no thoughts to spare for her. Another walk. The others looked at me in alarm. They all knew that prisoners are sometimes promised freedom simply in order to disturb the routine of their prison life and make them lose their nerve more easily when they are cross-examined again. None of us could know, of course, that my 'case' had been concluded in April, and that I had really been forgotten by the OGPU for four months.

Another dinner. How sick I was of it all!

Two o'clock. I lay down to rest. Perhaps the man really had changed his mind?

Three o'clock. The key was quietly turned in the lock and the wardress said:

'Get ready. Pack your things.'

These words may mean moving to another cell, going to be shot, or being released.

'Where is she going?' my neighbour cried excitedly.

There was no answer. The wardress stood by me while I packed my things.

'Be quiet!' she warned me, leading me out of the cell. It was all to be done secretly, but I wanted to give a treat to my neighbours, though I did not know them even by name: I stumbled, dropped my suit-case, and uttered an exclamation. That was my friendly greeting to give them hope that it was possible to leave this cursed house of the dead. The wardress shook her head reproachfully, but I was no longer in her power. The chief warder led me along the familiar gloomy corridors to the office with which my prison life began.

In the office all was dull and sleepy as before. A thin man instead of the fat one sat smoking and yawning. I was told to sit down on the bench and forgotten there. A good ten minutes passed. The thin man motioned carelessly to a dishevelled girl in a low dress, with painted lips and red-stained nails on her coarse, dirty fingers. She lazily handed him a book. He took a long time examining it. I was in no hurry either. I did not long for freedom. There can be no freedom in U.S.S.R. You go away from one prison to get into another, bigger one; you escape from the OGPU, but are surrounded in every place of work by its secret agents.

The clock ticked slowly on. At last I was handed a paper on which it said that I was kept in the House of Preliminary Detention from March, 1931, till August, 1931, that is, for more than five months. That was all.

'May I go now?'

'No, wait for the pass.'

Again they lazily wrote something out on a form and made an entry in a book. I recalled how one of my neighbours who indulged in fancies to escape from the misery of the prison asked me once:

'Tell me, would you walk through the town if they let you out naked? And if it were wet and cold and muddy?'

'Tarred and feathered,' I answered jokingly.

'No, don't laugh. I am serious. Or if they made you walk on all fours? It's silly, but I can't help thinking about it.'

She was a young woman and was imprisoned because her address was found at a dressmaker's who, in her turn, had been arrested on account of some other client. And indeed if the OGPU could keep a woman for six months in prison because in 1923 she had a skirt made for her by somebody who was arrested in 1931, they might with equal reason make her walk on all fours. But they like to give a bureaucratic form to all their absurdities. An official paper is all-important.

It was a quarter to four. It took them twenty minutes to write out my pass. I had to sign my name once more, and then the grated door of the prison was opened before me. But I went out with a heavy heart now that I knew by experience in whose hands lay the fate of us all.

CHAPTER XXIII

HOME

THE streets were hot and dusty. The windows of the Co-operative shops were completely bare. They were selling stale greens off the barrels. Passers-by looked tired and dull. In the tram passengers were quarrelling and abusing one another.

At home I found just what I had expected: strangers, disorder, most of the furniture sold. There was no home left — but all was made up to me by one cry that restored me to life:

'Mother!' It was a cry of ecstasy, tears, surprise, love, sorrow — all that was filling his childish heart.

'Mother, mother, mother!' he kept saying softly, loudly, caressingly, pitifully, in every tone of voice, finding no other words.

'Darling, why are you so pale and thin? Have you been ill?' I asked, examining him and feeling him all over. How wonderful it was that I could once more touch and stroke my poor abandoned boy.

'No, only once, a little. I had German measles, but I took your parcel to you just the same so that you wouldn't be worried. The doctor said I might. I had hardly any temperature, and when I came home I got into bed again.'

'Did you always take the parcels yourself both to me and to daddy?'

'Yes, I had to, there was no one else to do it.'

'How did you manage about school?'

'I missed two days a week and made up for it at home as best I could. You see, I had to go to two different prisons – you were at Shpalerka and daddy at Kresty. But it's ever so much nicer at Kresty. There are two windows there, one for parcels for ordinary prisoners – there are a lot of them there, and they can have all sorts of things – and another for the OGPU prisoners, and there they are awfully strict. But they are not so bad as at Shpalerka. They shout and swear at one, of course, but they don't drive one away so often. Mother, I am so glad I need not go to the prison any more! Mother, I shall never walk down that street again! You can't think how heavy those bags are, and I got so tired of standing in the queue! Mother, I am so glad you are back!'

He hugged me, kissed my hands, stroked me, rubbed his thin little face against me, and did not know how to express his joy.

'Where did you have your meals? You look so thin.'

'I had lunch at school, and in the evening I fed with our lodgers here. But they have very little money. There was jolly little to eat.'

'And where is my piano?'

'Sold. I was so sorry – now you won't be able to play in the evenings. I asked them very much not to sell it, but they said there wasn't any money to feed you. Parcels cost a lot, you know.'

The boy grew quite sad.

'Never mind, dearest. I shall have to work so hard now that there won't be time for music, anyway,' I said to comfort him, though I was very much grieved. All the time I was in prison I dreamed that perhaps I would be able to sit down to the piano again some day. But there was nothing for it! The OGPU might easily have confiscated all our property, and then we should have had nothing left us at all.

The boy's face remained sad and serious.

'I saw daddy.'

I could not speak; my voice failed me.

'When?' I brought out at last.

'In April. He was being sent to Kem.'

'What did he look like?'

'Very pale, and ill.'

'What did he say?'

'He said I was to go with you when you are sent into exile.'

There was a long silence. He was evidently making up his mind to speak. At last he asked:

'Shall we go to see daddy?'

'Yes. Soon.'

Now I knew what I had to do in life. There were only two creatures that I held dear in the whole world. We had to be together – at all costs.

·

CHAPTER XXIV

'INNER EMIGRATION'

IN prison I fancied that as soon as I was set free life would be full of absorbing work. I longed for work, and thought I would clutch at it greedily. Here I was free at last, and what did I do? I lay on the sofa and thought. Of my five months in prison, one was a means of bringing moral pressure to bear upon my husband, and four were the result of simple negligence on the part of OGPU officials. And I had once imagined that my work was of national importance!

In prison I suffered from lack of exercise: I felt like pacing up and down my cell that was six feet long; now I had attacks of exhaustion, felt giddy in the trams, and all I could do was to lie still, thinking of nothing – my head ached so dreadfully.

In prison I hated being waked at seven and wanted to be taken ill, so that at least I should not have to get up at that hour. Now I woke up at seven from a sense of acute anxiety which I could not control. It was probably the effect of my heart disease growing worse.

In prison I thought how lovely it would be to drink some good hot tea out of a china cup instead of an aluminium mug that burnt one's lips. Now I did not want to eat or drink.

I had lost taste for life – I did not want anything.

Or, rather, the only thing I wanted I could not do. I wanted to throw up everything and go to Kem. But through the wives of other convicts I learned that my husband was not at Kem; he had been sent for a time further north, no one knew where. I had to wait for news and look for a job. The house-committee informed me that if I did not get work I should not receive a bread-card, and my son would lose his – the unemployed were not allowed ration-cards now. That was something new.

My son, too, began to worry and asked: 'What about a job? When school begins, they'll ask me who is keeping me.'

'All right. I'll see about it.'

'Where will you go?'

'To the Hermitage. The examining officer said I was to go back to my old job.'

'Will they take you back?'

'I think not. When people are arrested their post is only kept open for two months.'

The boy walked with me thoughtfully to the Hermitage doors. We both loved the place; to him it was a fantastic, fascinating world, and to me my work there was my life. I specialised in French Art of the seventeenth and eighteenth centuries, and it was the only place where I could work.

'Wait for me on the quay, I won't be long,' I said, and went into the vestibule.

How familiar it all was – the stairs, the cloak-room, and all that filled the huge house that I loved so much. But my former colleagues looked at me uneasily – they did not know whether I was still one of them or a dangerous outsider.

I went to the director, Legrand. A former Soviet diplomatist, who disgraced himself in the Far East by drunkenness and scandalous love-affairs, he was made, as a punishment, director of the Hermitage. It certainly was a punishment for all the museum workers; he was very rude, and was hand in glove with the OGPU.

'What have you come for?' he asked me.

'I came because the examining officer told me to return to my old job.'

'Your place is taken and we don't want you any more.'

'Will you allow me to take my papers?'

'Go and take them. Wait a minute! Why did you spend so long in prison?'

'Ask the examining officer. His name is Lebedev. I have signed a promise not to speak about it.'

He shrugged his shoulders, and I walked out with a distinct sense of relief. That was over, and it was no good thinking about it. In the office I received my 'Work-list', something like a dossier without which one cannot obtain any post. Mine contained a record of all the posts I had held during the twenty-three years that I worked in the Commissariate of Public Education, and ended by saying that I was dismissed owing to my arrest. Had I kept my post for another two years I would have been entitled to a full pension, and now I did not know whether I could find work at all with such a 'ticket of leave'. On the card given me at the Hermitage office and marked 'specialist', I read that I had no right to look for work except through the Labour Exchange. So much the better, I thought: if, after twenty-three years work, they turned me out into the street for nothing, they might as well settle what I was to do.

'Well,' my son greeted me, 'did they turn you out?'

'They did.'

'Where shall we go now?' he asked sadly.

'To the Labour Exchange.'

'That's good!' He was glad that some way out presented itself. 'Come along, I'll see you off. But they won't send you to a stockings factory or a brick yard, will they?' he asked anxiously.

'No, I have a "specialist" card.'

'Come along, then.'

I had one friend and adviser now – my son. He was very grown up, thoughtful and practical, though he was only twelve and looked quite a child.

As though guessing my thoughts he said:

'Don't you worry! In another two years I'll finish school and will go to Fabzavutch.* They pay there and give one a 1st category ration-card. You won't have to go to an office then and can go to the Hermitage as much as you like to work on your own. Can't you?'

'Yes, certainly,' I said, not to disappoint him, though I knew that at Fabzavutch they paid only 20–30 roubles a month, and that I should never be able to take up my own subject again, because working for one's living meant a whole-time job.

At the Education Section of the Labour Exchange there were not many people – a few teachers and two girls who had just got their certificates for draughtsmanship. I gave the clerk my Work-Record. He read it, glanced at me in alarm, and began reading it again.

* A school attached to a factory.

'Excuse me, but where can I send you?' he said. 'You understand that workers with such qualifications as yours are never asked for at the Labour Exchange.'

'I quite understand. But I should like to find work through the Labour Exchange, as I am supposed to.'

'But I shall never be able to find the right sort of work for you!' said the young man with genuine concern. 'Perhaps you have some other speciality?'

'I am afraid I haven't,' I answered sadly. 'You see in another two years I would have got my pension.'

'But what else can you do?' he persisted.

It was an absurd position. I had worked for twenty-three years, I had been the senior assistant of the Curator of the Hermitage, formerly one of the best museums in Europe, and here I stood, wondering what I could do.

'Do you know any foreign languages?' he asked timidly.

'Yes, four modern and two ancient.'

He was again completely disconcerted.

'What shall I do with you? Where can I send you?'

'Send me to a most ordinary job, forget about the posts I once held.'

'But that would be a dequalification, and we mustn't allow that.'

'Well, in this case it isn't either your fault or mine.'

He ran out of the room to ask somebody's advice, came back, turned over all the papers on his table and ran off again. I watched him with interest. I knew that museums were short of staff, that my place at the Hermitage had been given to a girl who had just taken her final, and knew nothing about the work, and had no one to teach her – but what could I do? I had

devoted all my energies and all my knowledge to the
service of the State, and here I was, thrown out.

'I have an application from a library, but it is quite
simple work,' he said at last.

'So much the better, as I don't know library work
at all.'

'You can refuse it. If we offer you a job which is not
in your special line, you have a right to refuse it three
times.'

'But you know that I can't have a bread-card till I
find a job?'

'Yes that's so,' he answered shamefacedly.

'And so I thank you for your excellent suggestion. I
hope I shall give satisfaction and won't have to
trouble you again.'

In the institution where I was sent, my Work-Record
also produced a slight sensation, but I persuaded my
future chief to forget about it and believe that I would
do my work well.

'But why don't you try to find work apart from the
Labour Exchange?'

'Because if I am sent to you by the Exchange, you
risk nothing in taking me, but if an institution engages
me on its own initiative it may get into trouble for
helping me. Don't you see, though I was released from
prison, I was dismissed from my former post.'

'You are right.'

And so I became an obscure and conscientious
librarian. The work was easy. I did it quite mechanically, and left at four o'clock. My son was glad because
now I was never late coming home. 'Dequalification'
certainly had its advantages, but I could not help
feeling that I had been thrown overboard.

I was far from being the only one. After the 'sifting' in all educational institutions, numbers of people were turned out, chiefly because of their 'social origin', 'absence of proletarian psychology', and so on. They had to find new employment, in which their knowledge of foreign languages and general education could be of use. Thus, for instance, the only U.S.S.R. specialist in carved gems, graduate of a foreign University and author of learned monographs, became secretary to an engineer who was engaged in making musical instruments. A well-known architect was reduced to teaching mathematics. An excellent teacher took a job as proof-reader. Other specialists taught foreign languages, became draughtsmen, and so on. We were in the curious position of 'home *emigrés*' – an opprobrious term applied by the Bolsheviks to those whom they had themselves thrown out of employment. But whose fault was it? Everyone of us was longing to return to the work of which we had been so arbitrarily and senselessly deprived.

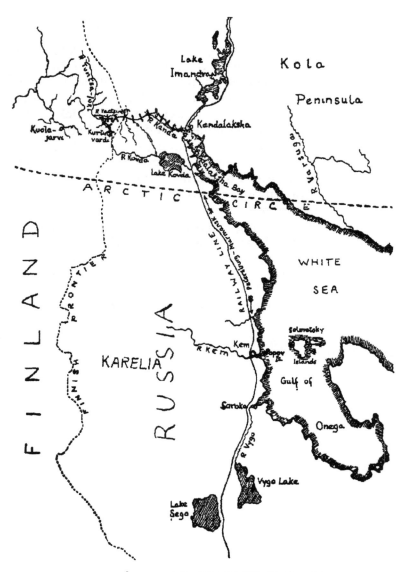

AUTHOR'S MAP SHOWING ROUTE OF ESCAPE

The Itinerary is denoted thus + + + + +

.

PART TWO

CHAPTER I

THE VISIT

TWICE a year a convict's relatives may apply for permission to see him. Permission may be given or it may not. Application must be made on the spot, and all the penal camps are in remote parts of the country. If permission is refused, they have to go back, not knowing whether they will ever see him again. They may be allowed to see him 'in the usual way', or, as an exception, be admitted 'on a personal visit'. The 'usual way' means that they may see him a certain number of times for two hours a day, between two and six, in the office, in the presence of an OGPU agent, who interferes in the conversation, forbids whispering, giving each other anything, speaking about life in the camps, about the details of the 'case', and about anything that strikes him as suspicious. 'Personal visit' is a rare piece of luck; it means that the convict is let off for several days to the 'free lodgings' where his family is staying. True, he has to go to work from eight in the morning till eleven at night, but *all the remaining time* and the dinner hour he may spend with his people, without being directly watched. Permission to see the prisoner at all, whether in the 'personal' or the 'usual way', and the length of time for which visits are allowed, entirely depends upon the arbitrary decision of the official in charge of the particular section of the penal camp in which the prisoner works; it is in his power, too, to cut short at any moment the visit for which permission has already been given.

I am not at all of an emotional temperament, but I confess that I completely lost my head when I finally decided to go. I felt exactly as though somebody had told me that I might see my father, who had been dead for seven years.

I had not seen my husband for over a year; during that year he had lived through his imprisonment, my imprisonment, had more than once been threatened with death, and from a free man had been turned into a convict.

The boy was so excited that we could hardly speak about his father and our visit to him. One morning he said to me that he did not feel very well, and would not go to school. When I returned he was in bed, but I guessed from his face that he had been up to something.

'Did you get up while I was away?'

'Yes.'

'Did you go out into the street?'

'Yes.'

'What for?'

The boy was no good at telling lies. Besides, he obviously had something on his mind that he wanted to tell me. Without answering, he bent down and fetched something rolled into a tube from under his bed.

'A map?' I asked.

'Yes,' he answered shamefacedly. 'I wanted to know exactly where daddy was, and how we would go to him. They gave me this huge map; there was no other. It cost three roubles, but it's my own money. Only I didn't think it would be so big.'

'And you didn't know where to hide it from me?'

'No. I thought you would be cross because I did not go to school. I would have shown you the map afterwards.'

Concealing my agitation, I sat down on his bed, helped him to unroll the map and, closely huddled together, we examined the green expanse indicating the marshes, the two big blue lakes – the Ladoga and the Onega, the black line of the railway that skirts round them and, beside a bay of the White Sea, a black point – Kem.

The boy kept rubbing his cheek against me, kissing and stroking me, glad that I understood and was not cross with him. As a matter of fact, I always did understand him, but when he was faced with something painful or difficult, he wanted to be left alone till he got over it. He declared that he was ill and spent the whole day in bed. That was what he did after his father's arrest – he lay in bed all the following day; he did not weep, nor complain, nor talk – he merely lay there thinking it over.

He was always delighted when I guessed what was on his mind, and said:

'Mother, how do you always know? You must be a bit of a witch, I think.'

'Of course. I know when you wash your hands without soap, when you don't clean your teeth, when you get out of bed.'

'And how do you know when I tell fibs?'

'Your nose always tells the truth.'

I caught him looking in the glass at his nice straight little nose, wondering how it could give him away.

We looked at the map, feeling exactly like the people who during the War tried to locate on the map of the front the trench where their loved ones were constantly facing death. Life in Soviet penal camps is no safer than being at the front.

After this incident we both felt a little better, but during the last few days before our departure we could scarcely speak for agitation.

'Mother, how shall we find daddy there?'

'I don't know.'

'Mother, when does the train get there?'

'At three in the morning.'

'What shall we do in the night?'

'I don't know. Perhaps the train will be late.'

'Mother, and will they let us see daddy?'

'I don't know, darling, I don't know. Don't ask me.'

We both thought of one thing only – of how we should find *him*. We had to take with us everything we should want there, because one could not buy anything at Kem, but we could only take as much as we could carry. I was warned that there were no porters at the station and no cabs, and it was two miles to the town. We made ourselves two hempen knapsacks to carry on our backs as peasants do.

The boy knew that he would have to rough it, and was not afraid, but he grew so tired with the excitement that he dropped fast asleep when he lay down to rest before the journey. The train left at one in the morning. I could scarcely wake him; he could not stand up, he was so sleepy.

'Wake up, darling, it's time to go.'

'Are we at the station?' he asked drowsily.

'Wake up. We shall be late. It's time to go.'

'Three o'clock?' he muttered.

'Not three, but half-past eleven. It's time. We are going to see daddy.'

He opened his eyes.

'To see daddy? Of course!' and he seized his huge bag, forgetting his cap and overcoat.

We dressed, slung our knapsacks on our shoulder, and went to the tram, trembling with cold and agitation.

There were hardly any cabs or taxis, and they were fantastically dear, quite beyond our means. I succeeded in selling a few things before going, but even so I had not enough money. The worst of it was I could not buy any galoshes for the boy, and the streets were wet and muddy. He had to wear his old ones that were in holes. I could not get him any gloves either, and he was wearing odd ones – one grey and one brown.

But nothing mattered if we only got there and saw *him*.

Here was the station – the former Nicolaevsky, then Octiabrsky, now Moscovsky; the Bolsheviks like to change names.

The Moscow train was the express, 'Red Arrow'; all the Soviet aristocracy and foreigners travel by it. We saw brightly-lit sleeping-cars and carriages with soft seats. The passengers had leather bags and attaché-cases. There were several Soviet ladies in sealskin coats with huge fur collars and the fashionable tiny hats.

The train for Murmansk-Kem left from a wooden side-platform. It was dark there and the place was seething with a democratic crowd with sacks, home-made boxes and enormous bundles from which worn boots and patched-up felt overshoes – the owners' last treasures – were sticking out. There were many peasants with saws and axes, many peasant-women with small children in tattered clothes, wrapped up in remnants of old shawls or simply in bits of rag. It was dreadful to think where they were going and what awaited them there. But the policy of exterminating the *kulaks* as a class, i.e., really of destroying all peasants who fail to fit into the collectivist scheme, has uprooted everyone. People wander over the whole of Russia, because in their native villages there is nothing but certain death to look forward to, and, though in distant parts it is death too, it is not so bad to die on the move. Many are driven out of their homes and deported; many go off of themselves in the hope that in some place they have vaguely heard of, people are given two and a half pounds of bread a day. Their ambitions do not rise beyond that. They do not know that those two and a half pounds of bread have been promised beyond the arctic circle, that they will have to live in dug-outs or in barracks which don't keep out the frost, that the children will all die in the winter – or if they do, they don't care. It's death either way.

The carriages are almost in darkness: there is no electric light, and only a bit of candle in a lantern burns dimly in each compartment. There are such

masses of people on the seats and on the shelves for
luggage that one sees nothing but heads and feet
everywhere. The space between the seats is taken up
with baskets, boxes and bundles on which sickly-
looking, dirty children sleep or sit in a kind of dull
stupor.

There is one 'soft' carriage (former II class) for the
important officials and the OGPU courier who has a
compartment to himself, and one 'hard' carriage with
numbered seats for the smaller officials and relatives
of the prisoners going 'on a visit' – if they can afford a
platzkarte.

When I was preparing for the journey I fancied that
I was the only one, but as soon as I entered the
carriage I at once saw people of my own sort. Nowadays people talk very little in railway carriages –
they exchange two or three words, and that's all: there
is no knowing to whom one may be talking, and
anything one says may be dangerous. It is not as in the
old days when everyone talked as hard as he could.
Now it is sufficient to say where you are going for
people to know what you are going for. Kem, for
instance – it has only some four thousand inhabitants
who have no occasion to go anywhere, and some fifteen
thousand prisoners; Mai-Guba is not even a village,
but it is one of the biggest centres for the convict
timber-works; Medvezhya Gora is the centre of a
penal camp much bigger than Solovki and the headquarters for building the White Sea-Baltic Canal.

Most of the officials got out at Petrozavodsk and
the remaining passengers began a conversation, the
essential part of which had no need to be put into
words.

'Are you going to Kem?' a thin elderly woman with a cough asked me.

'Yes. And you?'

'To Segozero.'

'Segozero?' I repeated, for the name was new to me.

'There's a new penal camp there. They say they are getting ready in case of war: the prisoners from Kem are being transferred to different points on the railway. There aren't any barracks even; they'll have to live all the winter in tents. I am bringing all the warm things I could collect. But a warm vest and two pairs of stockings won't save a man if he's got to live all the winter in the frost. They didn't begin building barracks till September and had only time to build two for the overseers. In the summer they will build barracks that will do for soldiers.'

'But where will you put up?'

'In the common tent. It's allowed because there is nowhere else to go – no village, not a single cottage, nothing. The camp is three miles from the station.'

'How will you get there? The train arrives at night, doesn't it?'

'At one in the morning. Oh, I'll just walk. It's all forest and marsh; there's no one about. I am an old woman. And if somebody did finish me off, I'd be only too grateful. I haven't any strength left. I am sorry for my boy, he isn't twenty yet, or else I shouldn't wait for death.'

'Why did they take him so young?'

'He was a student. I don't know what he had been up to, but suddenly they arrested him, said he was a Social-Revolutionary. He got three years of penal camps.'

'How long ago?'

'This is his second year. But what's the use of counting the years – they won't let him come home anyway. They'll call it "free exile" and send him to the Northern Urals or the depths of Viatka, where he'll be worse off than here.'

Looking at her more closely I found that she was not old at all. She might have been forty-five, but when she dropped asleep her thin, pale face framed with white hair looked so worn that she obviously had little hold on life.

'Have you other children?' I asked her. I felt dreadfully sorry for her and I did not know what to say to cheer her.

'No, I am all alone. My husband is dead. All my hopes were in my son. I am consumptive, and I am so afraid his lungs, too, will give way. Just think of it! He is nineteen; he was sent to the camp at eighteen and and imprisoned at seventeen. Social-Revolutionary! A dangerous political criminal at seventeen! He is a clever boy and was doing admirably at school. And the worst and dullest pupils, members of Komsomol,* denounced him to the OGPU saying he was not a Marxist and was opposed to the Soviet power. Ten boys were ̖arrested at the same time and sent to the camps. He won't live through it. Forgive me for worrying you with my troubles. I expect you have enough of your own.'

'Yes, I have.'

'Is it your husband?'

'Yes.'

'How long has he got?'

* Union of Communist Youth.

'Five years.'

'Grown up people stand it better than youngsters. You know it simply drives me mad coming here. To see one's son a convict! Good God, and what for? My one dream is to be allowed to stay with him. I would gladly be a convict too if only I could see him. But no! They let me see him for five or seven days and then I have to go back. I am so miserable, I don't know what to do with myself when I return to my work – teaching children just a little younger than he was when they took him. I feel that I teach them merely to prepare the more intelligent ones for penal servitude too! They can't bear people to have a grain of originality. . · '

She grew breathless, and after a moment's pause added quietly and hopelessly:

'I wanted to give up teaching and get a job in the post office, so that at least I need not see those boys – but the Labour Exchange won't let me. They haven't enough teachers to go round, and I have had long experience.'

I saw that the woman on the top bunk was listening. She differed from us two by being well dressed and looking rather like an actress, but the expression of her eyes, sad and thoughtful, made me at once guess that she was one of us.

'Do you remember Nekrasov's *Russian Women?*'* she asked, bending down to us. 'The luxury of it! The Emperor was angry, but those who wanted to join their husbands went. They lived there a real life,

---

* A poem about the wives of the Decembrists who followed their husbands to Siberia after the abortive mutiny of December, 1825.

Translator's note.

perhaps a better one spiritually than in Petersburg. They bore children. . . .'

'Don't you go in for monarchist propaganda!' I said jokingly.

'Is it your first visit?'

'Yes. It's not long since I've been released.'

'So they sent him away while you were in prison?'

'Yes.'

'You lucky woman! I understand how it is you can still joke. It's awful to see them like beasts in a cage. More than a hundred people in the room, all shouting, weeping. OGPU officials pacing up and down, shouting too – it's simply hell. And to see your husband there. . . . It's worse than death. And then to spend almost twenty-four hours in the street in front of the prison to see them being led out. . . . At the station to watch them, through the railings, being shoved into the train . . . oh! Why, to be in prison at the time is as good as being in a sanatorium!'

'Well, perhaps – if it were not for examining officers and the risk of being sent off too and leaving the boy alone.'

She raised herself on her elbow and glanced at the boy, who was fast asleep on the bench with his cap under his head.

'One can't have children in these times,' she said, looking at him. 'Forgive me, I was thinking aloud,' she added hastily.

'One can't live at all in these times,' the woman teacher answered.

We grew silent. The train rattled on. The old, shaky carriages creaked, the broken pane of the lantern kept clanking.

'Conductor, are we late?' asked a young, almost childish voice next door.

'We were two hours late, but we are catching up. Don't you worry, miss, I'll call you.'

'I am not a bit sleepy,' the girl's voice answered.

'Have you seen our neighbours?' the lady on the top bunk asked me in a whisper.

'No, why?'

'You go and look. A wonderful old woman.'

I went into the passage and sat down on the seat by the window, where I could see into the next compartment.

A tall old woman in a gorgeous black fur coat and a big black silk kerchief pinned over a Georgian velvet cap, sat there, leaning on a stick. Her hands were beautifully white, with heavy gold rings on her fingers and a diamond that sparkled with greenish fire when the light of the lantern fell upon it.

'Granny,' said a tall, slim girl, sitting down beside her. 'Granny, we shan't be there for another five hours. Do lie down!'

The old woman said nothing and did not stir.

'Granny, we shan't see mother till to-morrow morning. Do have a rest! I am not sleepy, but you will be tired out.'

The old woman sat there like a statue of sorrow and did not stir a finger.

The girl got up and folded her hands as in prayer.

'Granny . . .' her voice broke and she could say nothing more. The old woman raised her head suddenly, her sorrowful eyes flashed with anger, and she bent once more over her stick with a silver knob.

The girl buried her face in her hands and lay down. I went back to my place.

'Have you seen them?' the lady on the top bunk whispered. I nodded.

'A queen, isn't she? I keep fancying that she is the last queen of Georgia. My husband is a musician. I believe if he saw her he would set her to music. I can't do it. I feel it. I almost hear it, but I can't express it.'

'But what is your husband doing *there*?' I asked in surprise. I knew that actors were sometimes sent to penal camps, but musicians! Why?

'What is he doing? Playing. Amusing the authorities. Don't you know? There's a whole troupe there – musicians, singers, actresses, especially from the music-hall stage.'

'Forgive me, but . . . your husband, what reason could there be for convicting him?'

'He went to give concerts abroad.'

'And whom is the old woman going to see?'

'Her daughter. The girl told me. The father and mother are in a penal camp; there are only the two of them left. The grandmother had not spoken to anyone since her daughter was taken. And now she has said to the girl, "Let us go, I shall die soon", and so they are going. It's awful for the Georgians in those camps. They can't stand the climate, and all die either of consumption or pneumonia. The Armenians are stronger, but they don't survive it either. I've seen enough sights there.'

'Where are you going to now?'

'To Medvezhka. The headquarters have been transferred there and all the musicians, too. What does your boy think?'

'I don't know. I don't conceal anything from him, but I can't imagine how he really feels about it all. One blessing is that children live at a quicker rate than we do, and perhaps get over things more easily.'

'He is a fine boy – he hasn't said a word too much all the way.'

'We've taught him to hold his tongue.'

'What a life – one might as well be dead! That's a wise saying of my former maid. But the trouble is that we mustn't die.'

She soon had to get out and we parted like sisters. I felt uneasy about my other neighbour, who left the train at a deserted station in the middle of the night. Only the tragic old woman and her granddaughter were left in the train besides my son and me. The children slept: the old woman sat like an image of stone. I wrapped myself up as best I could and huddled up in a corner of the seat.

Kem. We were standing on an open platform made of planks; before us was a house built of logs with an inscription 'Station Kem'. What were we to do next? It was three in the morning and pitch dark. The earth was black and the sky was black too. There were a few lanterns on the platform, but night was all around us.

The boy looked at me with frightened, questioning eyes.

'Let us go into the station; it will be warmer there.'

People were going in and out of the creaking station-door and immediately disappearing in the darkness. We went in and drew back in alarm, but we were being pushed from behind, and so had to move forward. The whole place was completely filled with people, lying and sitting on their bags and wooden boxes. The foul-smelling air was thick and steamy. A small lamp was burning dimly under the ceiling. People were going through the room, stepping over those who slept on the floor. My son was frightened. He did not know how to move without stepping on someone. In the corner two men were quarrelling, on the point of a fight.

We managed to make our way to another room called the buffet. There were in it several dirty tables without tablecloths, broken chairs and a counter with two plates on it: one had treacle sweets in sticky papers and the other a few slices of black bread. There were fewer people here because those who did not ask for refreshments were driven out.

A fat attendant, sleepy and dishevelled, in a red kerchief and a short cotton skirt showing huge shapeless legs, was pouring out of a big kettle a brownish liquid made from baked oats; it was called coffee. The glasses were dull and sticky; there were no saucers. No sugar was to be had.

I took two glasses of the stuff, for anyway it was hot. The boy was trembling all over like a puppy after his sleep. We sat at our table, keeping a tight hold over our things for fear of thieves. Red Army men, civilians, and proud OGPU officials in long coats or leather jackets stood about the room.

A tall, healthy-looking peasant woman in a good coat and a woollen shawl sat down at our table.

'Have you come on a visit?' she asked, bending down to me.

'Yes.'

It was useless to deny it. Besides, I was not sure what I was to do and wanted to ask some questions.

'Tell me, please, when does the first motor-bus go?'

'The first bus? At eight or nine in the morning. Only it doesn't go at all now.'

'Why?'

'Broken down. It sometimes goes for a day or two, but you can't reckon on it.'

'How far is it to the town?'

'Two miles, but the mud is something awful. Will you wait here till morning?'

'I don't know. I've been told that a motor-bus meets the train?'

'It may do in the summer, but not at night, anyway. That doesn't matter. The road is wide and you can't go wrong, only it's muddy and dark. Is it the first time?' she asked me in a whisper.

'Yes.'

'Have you a permit?'

'What permit?' I asked in alarm.

'For the visit. The head office is at Medvezhka now and everyone has to go there to get the permit.'

I felt that all my plans were upset: I was given ten days leave from my office, the journey took more than twenty-four hours each way; I thought I would go in the morning to apply for the permit and perhaps see my husband in the evening – and what was I to do now? Had I known I would have stopped at Medvezhka that evening and lost twenty-four hours; if I went back now I might lose two or three days. And what was I to do with the boy? Take him with me? I hadn't enough money for the extra fares.

'Is it long since the head office was moved there?' I asked, as though that would help matters.

'No, only a week or two. Of course it used to be better for the visitors; now they have no end of trouble.'

'Is there an hotel here?'

'Yes, there is that. Only there's never any room. Communists and officials live there, and visitors can hardly ever get in. And it's dear, too – 2 roubles 50 copecks for a bed in the common room and 4 roubles in a separate room. For the three of you they'll charge 12 roubles.'

At that moment an OGPU official appeared in the doorway; the fat attendant shouted in alarm to the people in the room:

'Clear out, I am going to close.'

'Why, what has happened?' I asked someone in the crowd; they were all making for the door.

'It's the rule. The buffet opens for half an hour when the train comes in and then shuts again.'

Once more the boy and I found ourselves on the dark platform. There was not a soul about. The train had gone and the place seemed darker and more deserted than ever. It was unthinkable to stay in the station room – it was filthy and stuffy and there were sure to be lice. It was four in the morning – another three and a half hours till dawn. We had to wait.

We sat down on a bench, putting our things down beside us.

'Mother, what shall we do?' the boy asked anxiously. 'Who is this woman. Do you know her?'

'No, how should I?'

'But you talked to her!'

'I had to – you see how things have turned out: there

is no bus, no room at the hotel, and permits are not given here.'

'And you were told it would be all right! Who told you?'

'They told me what it was like a month ago; now it's all different. When it's light we must go to the town and find out what exactly we have to do.'

'Mother, I am simply frozen.'

'Run about the platform to get warm.'

He ran up and down the platform while I sat by the luggage, also shivering.

'Mother, I am still cold; my feet are like ice. When shall we go to the town?'

'When it is light – in another three hours.'

'I'll be quite frozen by then!'

'Run about, keep on the move.'

I was afraid the boy would catch cold. What was I to do? Perhaps we had better start – anyway, we should be warmer. But where could we put up?

When I was in absolute despair, the peasant woman who had talked to me appeared again and sat down beside me.

'Your little lad must be quite frozen,' she said.

'He is, but what's to be done?'

'Look here, citizen, I don't know if you'd care to come, but I always take in visitors. I have a nice house in the main street. In the morning your man will have to go past us; you will see him.'

'May we come now?' I asked.

'Yes, certainly. Call the lad. We'll settle up after-wards. You won't take advantage of me.'

I called the boy.

'Come along!'

'Where to? Mother, what are you doing?'

'It's all right, dear, come, or you'll get your death of cold.'

'Never you mind, sonny, put on your bag, it will keep you warm,' the woman said.

She took my bag, the boy slung on his, and we set out on the muddy road. It was so dark that we could see nothing underfoot. There were no street lamps. At a distance there were some buildings with lighted windows, but we could not make out their outline against the dark sky.

The woman chatted away.

'I never went to bed at all last night,' she told us. 'I had a visitor. She too had come to see her husband, such a nice woman, in a lovely overcoat, and good clothes, and so young and pretty. Her husband had got ten years, she said, and quite a young man too. It's no joke! Every time she looked at him she began to cry, and I cried looking at her. So it was nothing but tears. I am a widow, but I do understand how dreadful it is for them. The numbers of people they ruin! It doesn't bear thinking about. How many years has your husband got?'

'Five.'

'That's not so bad, one can live through it. But there's a lot of sickness about, scurvy, and typhus too. You send him parcels, don't you?'

'Yes, I do.'

'You must go on doing that, or he'll be sure to die if he gets scurvy or consumption. So many of them die of consumption. . . . I've just seen my visitor off,' she went on with her story, 'and I was sitting there wondering what to do. I don't like walking home alone in the night. Then I saw you and your boy and thought you must have come on a visit.'

'Are there many visitors?' I asked, completely re-assured by what she told me. I had been feeling a little uneasy going with a complete stranger to a place I knew nothing about.

'Yes, a great many. They come every day and walk about the village asking to be let in for Christ's sake. One can't take in anyone – there's the house to con-sider, and one's clothes and other things lying about; and the visitors bring in a lot of dirt too. The OGPU are cross because we take in visitors and don't let rooms to them. But why should we? They don't pay more than three roubles a month and they spy on one all the time. Don't you tell them that I let you in. You'll have to give your address, but you must say that I am a friend and put you up in the kitchen.' She paused and asked the question that had evidently been troubling her: 'Will you pay me three roubles a day?'

'Yes, certainly.'

'Then you're very welcome,' she said, evidently pleased. 'I've got a bed and I'll heat a samovar for you.'

We were very tired and could hardly keep pace with the woman. She strode along in a man's top boots, tucking up her skirt and overcoat above her knees. My feet sank in the mud up to the ankle, but I had overshoes on; the boy's feet must have been wet through.

We were almost exhausted by the time we reached the town; even our landlady became subdued. It is difficult to walk when one can't see. In the town we soon found ourselves in the main street, which stretched a very long way because the town, or rather, the fishing village, was built along the winding shore of the bay. The wooden houses were typical of the rich north country villages: they had two stories and were divided into two parts, 'the living-rooms' and the 'clean' part, meant for the summer.

'The OGPU,' said the woman in a whisper, pointing to a large house of grey stone with big windows. It was in the new style but beautifully designed. One could see at once that it was the work of a fine architect.

'Is it much further?' the boy asked impatiently.

'Quite near now, sonny. Come, let me take your bag.'

She flung the second bag over her shoulder and walked still faster so that we had almost to run to keep pace with her. My one thought was not to fall down into the mud.

At last she stopped before a tall wooden gate and opened it by pulling a string. A dog barked furiously.

'Don't be afraid, he doesn't bite. He smells strangers.'

At the door of the house she pulled another string, and going through the dark entry opened the door of the kitchen. The dog rushed forward, barking desperately, but did not attack us.

The kitchen was a large room with a low ceiling. By the back wall there was a big white-washed Russian stove; narrow wooden benches ran alongside the other three walls; above the small windows there were narrow shelves full of beautifully polished copper dishes, basins and mugs of the ancient Russian pattern. A huge copper pan, like a gigantic vase, stood by the stove. There were spotless white curtains over the windows, edged with home-made lace. Narrow homespun runners were spread on the wooden floor, clean as a table.

The whole place was so clean that one was afraid to take a step.

An old woman in a black, flower-patterned sarafan, an embroidered head-dress, and a dark apron tied above her waist, was busy by the stove.

'Brought some visitors?' she asked, glancing at us with interest.

'Yes, from the station.'

'Shall I heat a samovar?'

'Do, they are very tired. Well, you are welcome!' she turned to us, inviting us to come in.

'Take off your shoes, sonny,' the old woman said. 'Come and warm yourself by the stove.'

He hastily took off his coat, galoshes, shoes and socks that were soaked through with mud and joyfully walked barefoot to the stove.

After the noisy, dirty train, the filthy station, the cold and the darkness outside, it seemed incredible to be in this clean warm room smelling of freshly-baked bread. Everything here was the same as it had been for centuries.

The inner room was also extremely clean. On the wooden bed there was a cotton eiderdown and big down pillows with a white lace coverlet over them. The table was covered with a crotchetted cloth; there were a few chairs and a big case with ikons. There were pots of flowers in the windows and a tropical plant in the corner. Everything was as it should be, and the same as it had been for ages.

'Come and have some tea,' the landlady called us.

On the kitchen table a big copper samovar was boiling; a tiny teapot with a blue and gold pattern stood on the top. In a sugar basin of coarse bluish glass were a few tiny lumps of sugar. The old woman was taking hot scones out of the oven.

While we were drinking tea it began to grow light. Quick, loud footsteps sounded on the wooden pavement outside.

'That's the prisoners,' the landlady said. 'Now sit down by the window and look; your man also will soon go past. Where does he work?'

'At the Fisheries.'

She cleared the table and prepared to do some washing. I sat by the window and the boy leaned against me. We both looked out without speaking; I could feel his heart beating fast, and mine was throbbing too.

An endless procession of men and women was moving along the narrow wooden pavement and the wide street covered with sticky mud. They did not look like ordinary people, poor or rich, sad or cheerful: they all seemed alike and had the same set, strained expression. All hurried along in silence. They were strangely dressed: all had some 'convict' garment – short trousers or a reddish coat or a cap with ears, but nearly all were also wearing some of their own things – a shabby beaver cap, worn town-shoes, a coat with an astrakhan collar with no buttons on, belted with a strap off a suit-case. Women were dressed with more care; almost all had knitted caps or berets, many had woollen scarves, but almost all were wearing men's coats and top boots much too big for them.

'Why are they dressed like that?' I asked the land-lady.

'They have to wear what is given them, and there aren't enough things to go round. And they are wearing out what is left of their own clothes.'

It was obvious from the faces, the manner, the clothes, that practically all of them belonged to the educated class. One does not come across such a mass of intellectuals either in Moscow or in Petersburg.

'So here are the experts whom the country so badly needs!' I thought. 'Those will not return to life after five or ten years forced labour here. . . . No. It is enough to look at their faces.'

'How is your man dressed?' the landlady asked.

'He has a brown leather coat.'

'Ah, then, he will soon go past,' she said confidently. 'Those who work in the Fisheries come later; there are thousands of them; it takes nearly an hour for them all to go down the street. They go to offices in the town or to work-rooms. They are not so badly off as the others. But those who do the common work, make roads or cut timber, have to go before dawn, poor things. They go in batches under escort, and those who work in the town are allowed to go by themselves. They are checked in the barracks before they go out, that's all. Not much chance of their running away! There are swamps all round. And besides, everyone has a family at home – if he runs away, they'll seize the family. Ordinary criminals do run away; it's nothing to them; if they are caught, their sentence is increased, that's all. But if a decent man runs away he is shot. Sonny!' she called to my boy, 'put on your things and go into the street. Walk to meet your

father, but when you see him take no notice of him –
they are not allowed to speak to outsiders. Go past
him so that he can see you and then turn back and
overtake him. Walk in front of him and listen to what
he says. He may have applied for a permit for you,
and perhaps he's had an answer.'

The boy dressed and ran out. I saw out of the
window that he did not venture at first to go against
the current among all this mass of people, but presently
he made up his mind and walked slowly on. Almost
all the women turned to look at him, but the set look
on their faces did not change – he came from another
world which it is too painful to recall. That was how I
felt in prison. Many men, too, turned and looked at
him as they walked past.

'Is your boy all right?' the landlady asked. 'One must
be careful; there are no end of spies about. If they say
that he spoke to a prisoner you won't be allowed to
see your husband.'

'Yes, he understands.'

I was in a perfect fever. I was just going to see him.
There he was! He was walking fast, faster than the
others. His face was pale and he had grown a black
beard. His hands were thrust in his pockets, his head
thrown back as usual. He saw me, nodded and went
on faster than before.

I sat there not seeing anything any more. The
hurried footsteps of the late comers sounded in
the street, and soon all was still. The street was
empty.

The gate banged; my little boy walked in slowly, as
though he were in pain. He came up to me and hid
his face in my lap.

The old woman was muttering something to herself and wiping her eyes with her apron.

I raised his head. He was not crying, but his first encounter with the convicts left its shadow on his childish face.

'What did daddy say?'

'He said you must go at ten to the commandant's office. Permission has been received.'

'What else?'

'Nothing.'

He again hid his face in my lap. After a while he recovered and said:

'It's time to go.'

'It's a bit early yet, but we may as well.'

Our landlady told us how to get there. It was in the same street: the OGPU headquarters on one side, the militia-station opposite, and the commandant's office next door to it. We set off.

By daylight the town seemed still smaller; if it were not for the new house of the OGPU all would be calm and peaceful and, in places, beautiful – where one could see the curving line of the shore and the deep bay dotted with small islands. But the whole landscape suggested the desolate North.

We came to the commandant's office: a narrow passage, a wooden partition with a window in it. Behind the window sat an OGPU official, a huge, well-fed creature with a fat, ruddy face and their usual blank expression. They must be specially trained to look like that.

'Where do I get permission for a visit?' I asked him.

'The permits office.'

'My husband wrote to me that he has applied for a permit, so perhaps it has already been granted.'

'The permits office.'

He shut the window with a click. There was no one about whom I could ask where the 'permits office' was.

We came out into the street. The few passers-by looked like convicts, and I was afraid to speak to them for fear of getting them into trouble.

'Where shall we go now, mother?'

'Let us go to the OGPU.'

We looked at the house. On the ground floor there had been shops and a hairdresser's salon, now closed. Evidently everything had been transferred to the new headquarters at Medvezhka because it only existed for the needs of the higher officials. The entrance was round the corner. On the first floor there was a large office with a wooden partition across and a window in it; over it was written 'Permits'. Two elderly shabby-looking women of the educated class, a peasant woman with a baby, and a lady in a seal-skin coat were standing there waiting. The lady was soon called to the inner office.

The shabby intellectual in front of me whispered to the other:

'Her husband is a Communist; he was exiled for opposition. He has an important post here too, but the non-party men who served under him in Moscow have all been shot.'

Behind the window was a youngish man whose hopeless expression made me guess at once that he, too, was a prisoner. He spoke in a very low voice.

'How do I get a permit for a visit?'

'You must fill up a form.'

'But my husband has applied already, so perhaps the permit has been received?'

'You must fill up a form,' he said in the same low, even voice.

I knew that I was doing the wrong thing, or perhaps had come to the wrong window. From the other women's conversation I gathered that one of them had been waiting for a permit for a week and another for ten days. Their applications had been sent to Medvezhka, but there was no answer from there.

I filled up the form. The boy was obviously upset, but said nothing till we came out into the street.

'Mother, but daddy said you must go to the commandant's office and get the permit.'

'But, my dear, you've heard what the commandant said?'

'And daddy said it would be all right.'

'Let's go there again, but mind, we must not let out that you've seen daddy.'

We came to the commandant's office again.

'Excuse me, but they sent me to you from the permits office,' I lied at random. 'Perhaps you have already received the permit?'

'No.'

'What am I to do then?'

'Wait.'

'Where am I to inquire?'

'At the permits office.'

The window was shut. A queue was standing there by now, and they grumbled at me for coming to the wrong place.

We went out into the street. The boy's eyes were full of tears.

'Go home,' I said to him.

'I won't go anywhere till you get the permit.'

'But how am I to get it?'

'You keep saying the wrong thing.'

'I'll go once more to the permits office and then you can go and talk to the commandant yourself.'

He remained in the street and I went up to the office.

'Tell me, what am I to do?' I said quietly to the hopeless young man.

'Wait for an answer to your application,' he said aloud, and then added in a whisper: 'Call in the evening.'

That gave me hope anyway. I went into the street again and told the boy. He was unhappy at the delay and thought that I did not know how to set about the business. But I knew the habits of the OGPU: it was quite possible that the permit was lying at the commandant's office, but he did not want to give it me straight away; it was possible, too, that they had deceived my husband and that there was no permit, and would not be. Men who have unlimited power and no responsibility whatever do many things for no reason at all.

'Let us go and look at the Fisheries,' said I. 'Perhaps daddy will see us.'

We walked the whole length of the street and turned back again. We felt utterly miserable.

Suddenly we heard the familiar, nervous footstep behind.

'Have you got the permit?' he asked without stopping. I shook my head.

'Go to the commandant's office,' he said, walking on in front.

'There, you see!' the boy said triumphantly.

My husband walked fast and came to the office before us; we followed him in.

'You see, my wife and son have come to see me. I have been promised a permit, perhaps it has been given to you?'

We stood in silence, not daring to go near him.

'You may talk,' the commandant said in the same stony voice, and shut the window.

We sat down on the bench by the window. We did not speak, but just held hands. The boy was stroking his father's hand, his knee, his coat.

'Did you recognise me with a beard?' his father managed to say at last.

'I did,' the boy answered seriously. 'You smoke a pipe now?'

'Yes. How do you know?'

'Why, you have a pipe in your pocket.'

How strange it was. . . . His face was the same and yet not the same. What ages had passed since we last looked at each other! It might have been in another existence. He used to be handsome – they are a good-looking family – he was handsome still, but what a face! Whom did he remind me of? Oh, yes, Surikov's picture, *Streltsi before the Execution.* He was terribly pale, and his skin was coarsened by the wind and the cold. There were shadows under his eyes and under the cheek-bones. The untrimmed black beard made him look as though he belonged to some other age. His neck was dreadful: thin and withered, it showed above the collar of an old thick shirt with strings instead of buttons, and it seemed as though the head were too heavy for it. His hands too were rough and terribly thin.

When a year ago they took him to prison, he was a young man: though he was forty-two he easily passed for thirty-five. Though he could not be called old now, it was clear that he had not long to live.

The window opened.

'Citizen, your passport.'

I gave it.

'Here is your permit for the visit. Sign. You'll receive your passport back when the visit is over.'

I signed and carefully put away the permit. Prison had taught me not to show any feelings before the OGPU officials, but I felt as though a weight had been lifted off my heart.

Now we walked down the street together. My husband held the boy's hand, and I walked beside them. He had huge boots on and walked in the mud, as though it were the natural thing to do. Our son, forgetting everything in the world, tried to keep pace with him, chattering away. He talked of his school, of the journey, of me, of how he did not let me go anywhere alone now for fear I would be 'lost' – of everything he could think of. I could see that his father was not taking in his words, but merely listening to the child's voice. The boy was bubbling over with joy because he was holding his father's hand and talking to him, while only half an hour before everything had seemed so hopeless.

'How stupid of me to make you walk in this mud!' said his father, noticing that I was lagging behind. 'I am used to it. Till quite recently we were forbidden to walk on the causeway so I've lost the habit of it.'

'That's nothing, daddy, I don't like walking on the

causeway, and it's not very muddy here,' the boy said with conviction, getting another galoshful of liquid mud.

'Where are we going? Where did you put up?' my husband asked. 'It was so dreadful that I could not do anything for you. We are kept in the camp behind barbed wire and are not allowed to speak to anyone in the town. I simply did not know what to do – and the train arrives at night, too.'

'Everything turned out splendidly,' I reassured him. 'We've put up with some townspeople, very nice women.'

'The townspeople are very nice. It's much better than in the hotel, of course, there it's full of spies. But I can't come with you now. I must go back to work. I've been let off on business,' he remembered suddenly.

'How? Daddy, darling, why?'

The boy and I were so grieved that he gave in, though perhaps it was not safe for him to do so.

'I'll call in for a minute, then go to work and return by four o'clock; the day will soon pass.'

We said nothing. It was dreadful to feel all the time that he was a slave.

'It's a wonderful piece of luck that I got the permit before you arrived and that we met so soon,' he said to comfort us. 'People often have to wait a week or ten days, and then are only allowed to meet at the office. And at the Solovki Islands visits are hardly ever allowed.'

We went in at the gate. The boy was amused at the way it opened: you pulled a string, and that was all. His father followed him more and more timidly. I saw that he had lost the habit of houses and that being constantly forbidden to do this and that had unnerved him.

'Come in, daddy. This is the kitchen and the next room is ours.'

The boy had forgotten all his fears. He was happy at being with his father and at the moment wanted nothing more. All was right with the world.

We went into the kitchen, but my husband stopped irresolutely by the door. He certainly did look peculiar: his huge boots of coarse leather clattered as though they were made of stone; his once excellent leather coat was stained, the pockets were torn, the buttons broken or missing; his fur cap was worn and shabby. Holding it in his hands, he shyly bid good morning to our landlady.

'Good morning, you are welcome,' said the woman. 'Come into the inner room.'

'I am very dirty, look at my boots. . . .' He could not bring himself to walk on the freshly-washed floor and the clean bright-coloured runners.

'Oh, that's nothing; it's easily washed off. I haven't yet cleaned the place this morning. Look at the mess the hens have made, a perfect disgrace; excuse me!'

She started catching the hens and the cock who was proudly strutting about the kitchen.

'Wipe your boots with the broom,' said the old woman, coming to my husband's rescue.

Sitting down on the narrow bench, he carefully wiped his boots and walked cautiously to the inner room.

His movements were different from what they used to be – slow and awkward; perhaps because he found it so unusual to be in a house.

In our room he quietly shut the door behind him and held out his hands to us. That was how we stood when he said good-bye to us before going to prison. The bitter sorrow of all we had been through during that awful year suddenly rose up within me. . . . I wanted to be glad – and could not. I wanted to tell him how, in prison, I had lived in the thought of him, how I had longed to see him – and I could not find a word. I wanted to smile and I saw that his eyes were full of tears.

'Daddy, darling, don't cry,' the boy whispered, stroking his hand. 'You see, we have come to you, and we will come again, poor darling daddy.'

We kissed each other and sat down.

'Daddy, would you like something to eat? We've brought all sorts of nice things for you. Will you?'

'No, thank you, dear,' his father answered affectionately, gradually recovering his self-control. 'It's time I was going.'

'When is your dinner hour?' I asked.

'At four.'

'And you begin work at eight?'

'Yes.'

'Have you nothing to eat till four?'

'No. Yes. We sometimes have something to eat before beginning work.'

'What do you have?'

'Oh, something out of our parcels from home – those who get parcels.'

'And those who don't?'

'They have bread.'

'How much?'

'A pound.'

He was looking at me affectionately as he answered, and was obviously not thinking of the dreadful conditions in which he lived. I was questioning him with the burning hatred that was born in me while I was in prison and flared up again when I saw the convicts hurrying to their work.

'Is the dinner worse than in prison?' I persisted.

'Yes, it is,' he answered absent-mindedly with a smile.

'What do you get?'

'Oh, for dinner. . . . Well, we don't return to dinner. They give you a mug of soup, worse than any slops: smelly bits of salted horse or camel flesh or rotten cabbage in muddy-looking water. Disgusting. The prison dinner is a luxury by comparison.'

'But how do you manage, then?'

'As a great favour we've been allowed to receive dry rations. We do our own cooking.'

'What do you cook?'

'Oh, anything. Millet porridge.'

'There's scurvy in the camps, isn't there?'

'Yes, scurvy, too. Onion and bacon are badly needed. But I expect it costs a lot?'

'No, not much. I've brought you some and will send some more when we get back.'

'I don't need any for myself. I have some left from your other parcels. I've been saving it.'

'Why? How silly!' I said angrily.

'Don't be angry,' he said gently, taking my hand. 'You see, I don't know what you are living on, how you manage. It will be many years before I can do anything for you.'

'Well, go on. Do you return to the barracks at four?'

'Some of us have now been allowed not to return, but to remain at work.'

'I suppose that's a favour, too?' I asked, unable to control my irritation.

'Of course it is. The work-rooms are also crowded, but it is warmer and cleaner there. The barracks are rather awful: a thousand people herded together, and two rows of wide shelves, one above the other, to sleep on.'

'When do you rest?'

'We eat at four o'clock and have a little sleep.'

'Where?'

'On the floor, sometimes on the table.'

'When do you stop work?'

'At eleven at night. Then we go into the barracks. At midnight we are checked. Those who work in the forest or dig the canal are much worse off,' he added in the same calm, gentle voice. 'They have to begin work at six in the morning and go on without any break till dark. I was there first, carrying timber, but afterwards they put me in the Fisheries, because I am a specialist. And my health gave way, too.'

'What was the matter with you?'

'Myocarditis and . . . my lungs,' he answered rather shyly.

A nice state they've reduced him to! I thought indignantly. And he had once been so strong. This was after one year. How much longer would he last? A year? Two years? No, certainly not two.

'But I am afraid I must go,' he said apologetically. 'I don't want to get into trouble just now. Perhaps they'll let me off early. I will soon be back.'

'Come along, daddy, I'll walk with you,' said the

boy, who had been holding his father's hand all the time and hanging on his every word.

They went away; I remained sitting where I was.

'Excuse me for troubling you,' said the landlady, coming in quietly, 'but would you mind going and registering yourself? It's not far to go. If you don't the OGPU is sure to turn up here in the night. There's nothing they like better – that's their living.'

'I am so sorry, I'll go at once.'

'Mind you don't tell them that you have a room; say you put up in the kitchen.'

'Yes, certainly.'

I came out into the street again. There were no passers-by except an occasional OGPU agent, sleek and well groomed, in a smart long coat of military pattern. A queue was standing outside the vodka-shop. An old woman going past grumbled at them:

'Glad of the nasty stuff, aren't you!'

'Take your turn in the queue, granny!'

'No ration-cards needed, it isn't bread.'

'We've been fasting long enough, only the OGPU shop has had vodka to sell.'

'The OGPU are sure to have all they want, they are the Soviet gentry!'

'In the old days we hadn't any gentry in these parts and now they've sent us the new sort.'

The queue grew more lively.

A tall OGPU agent who stood on point duty in the street, took a few steps towards the queue. There was instant silence. When he was out of earshot one of the men muttered:

'He's got sharp ears, the cur! Spying on the prisoners isn't enough for him!'

I went into the militia-station: the doors were open, the dirty staircase was littered with cigarette ends. The corridor, equally dirty, was dark. There was nothing to direct one anywhere. It was a familiar scene. A yellow-faced official sat at the table. I laid my permit before him; my passport had been taken from me, so that I was a kind of hostage for my husband.

'Register me, please.'

'Have you a permit?'

'What other permit do you want?' I was angry and behaved in the Soviet style.

'To hire a room?'

'I haven't hired a room, I put up at a friend's house in the kitchen.'

'Bring me the permit.'

'Where from?'

'Table number five.'

'Number five, indeed! I can't find another room in your place.'

'It's next door, come this way,' said the official more politely, taken aback by my defiant tone. Everyone comes here as a humble supplicant.

In the next room there was a young man of Communistic appearance in a leather jacket.

'Give me a permit for registration,' I said in the same tone.

'We do not allow visitors to hire rooms in the town, there is an hotel for the purpose.'

'Twelve roubles a day? I earn a hundred and twenty roubles a month and have a child to keep. I have put up in the kitchen of someone I know.'

'I won't give you a permit, citizen.'

'I will complain to the OGPU.'

I was exasperated and did not care any more. The Communist probably did not want to have an explanation with his superiors, so he gave me the permit and I was registered.

'They behave like scoundrels about every little thing,' I thought. 'They are used to people kotowing to them. Well, I shan't.'

At home – that is, at the cottage where we found shelter and which I shall remember gratefully to my last hour – I sat down by the window again and watched the street.

A party of young but extremely exhausted-looking men went by. Their faces were grey, their heads and shoulders bent as though under some terrible weight, though they were carrying only half-empty sacks. They were surrounded by an armed escort.

'They are being sent to dig the new canal,' said the old woman with a sigh and made the sign of the cross over them. 'The Lord save and preserve them, and have mercy upon us! I wonder if any of them will come back alive? Fresh parties are sent along every day and there are no barracks there, no tools to work with – they say, they have to dig with wooden spades, and the earth is hard as stone with the frost. If a man doesn't dig as much as is fixed for him he loses his ration; and the ration is only one pound of rye bread and soup with bits of rotten meat in it. And he isn't allowed to sit by the fire, but must stay behind, in the forest. When the frost gets stronger in the night they freeze to death. Many envy them, and no wonder.'

The old woman finished washing up, put away the clean plates, cups and spoons on the shelf, drew a clean white curtain over it and sat down beside me.

'Tell me, my dear, why has all this happened? Maybe you are a learned woman and know.'

I shook my head.

'You don't know?'

'No.'

'That's just it – no one seems to know. If one knew, perhaps one might do something about it. The old women say the devil is to blame, but I think it's men's own doing. Some men are worse than the devil.'

'Of course, it's men's own doing, granny.'

'Men are destroying one another, and why? There's room enough for all. We had plenty of everything in the old days – fish, and bread, and we baked scones and pies every day. And we drank coffee, too – the Norwegians brought it over, and our men went by sea into their country. This used to be a rich part. Nearly all the women wore pearls. We have river pearls here, you know.'

'Do you get them now?'

'Not likely! They are not easy to find and we couldn't sell them – they would be taken from us for nothing. The women who had any, lost theirs – taken to the treasury, they said. Treasury indeed! The OGPU hussies wear them. And what fine clothes we had!' the old woman went on with her reminiscences. 'Gold brocade bodices and lovely wide skirts, all sorts of colours, like flowers. On Sundays the girls used to walk down the street and the women sat by the gate. Not much pleasure going out now! only the fat OGPU men stroll about. The young men have all gone where best they could. If they stay here they're sent to the timber works.'

Two carts slowly drove down the street. Something

long, covered with sacks and strips of tarpaulin lay on
them. A sudden jerk made the covering slide off,
baring the head of a man who was obviously uncon-
scious; the body of another, lying next to him jolted
against him.

'What is that, granny?' I cried in horror, clutching at
the old woman's hand.

'Don't be alarmed, my dear, they are still alive. They
are men from the canal-works, sick with typhus. There
is no hospital there, so they bring them here. There's a
lot of typhus among them. But what's the good of
bringing them here? They'll die anyway. The Lord
help them and have mercy upon us! Go away from the
window and put yourself to rights,' she said decisively,
drawing the curtain. 'Your man will come and you
don't look yourself. You'll see nothing good here.'

The old woman was wise. I went to do my hair and
make myself tidy.

My son came in. Lucky boy, he saw nothing but his
father. He had yearned for him with all his childish
heart and was happy at having found him at last.

'Mother, have you got the food ready? What shall we
give daddy? I am soon going to meet him. You know, I
saw X, – he recognised me. I did not speak to him but
simply looked at him, and he walked past me and said
"good day". I thought there would be only strangers
here, but there are lots of people I know! Well, get
everything ready, I'll go now.'

He ran away. I put the food on the table: butter,
ham, a cold fowl, white bread, cheese. I bought all this
at the cost of an eighteenth-century set of china and a
collar of Alençon lace. So long as the OGPU, the
flying corps and the heads of the Red Army have all

they want, it is possible to buy things, of which ordinary citizens do not even dream. True, there was very little left of my collection of china, but I no longer cared. I wanted to have something that day to remind us of ordinary civilised life.

We felt more light-hearted at our second meeting; the sorrow of all we had been through was giving way to joy. We were sitting at table, the three of us, we were eating together. It is such a simple thing, but it had seemed utterly unattainable when death was threatening at least one, if not two, of the three.

The child was delighted with our festive meal: he had not tasted anything so good during the whole of that terrible year. My husband ate absent-mindedly, smiling happily as he watched the boy. He himself had very little to eat and said that he had had enough.

'Enough! You've only had two sandwiches! Daddy, what's the matter with you?'

'The sandwiches were with butter and ham, and I had a piece of fowl, too. I've lost the habit of eating such things.'

'Did you have to go hungry?' the boy asked, and left off eating.

'Yes, it was pretty bad. But I am better now. They sent me to investigate the OGPU Fisheries on the White Sea.'

'By yourself?' I asked in surprise.

'Yes, but they gave me a boat and a net.'

'That was all your "technical equipment"?'

'Yes. But I've done a good deal, all the same. I went all over the western shore of the White Sea. It's strange,' he added, after a pause, 'whatever conditions we are placed in, our mind goes on working all the

same. I believe I've made an interesting scientific
discovery. . . . I should like to write about it, but I
won't be allowed to publish anything while I am here,
so I don't know what to do. . . . Are there as many
arrests as ever?'

'Not quite. And indeed I don't know who there is left
to arrest.'

'Oh, they'll find them.'

'That's true, though. They've started on translators
now. One of them was arrested for having translated
Marcel Proust – "a decadent writer"! And of course
the translation had been ordered by the Government
Publishing Office.'

We did not want to talk of prison and exile, we
longed to banish if only for a moment the bitter and
humiliating memories but we could not; nothing
remained of the happy past – and our present was the
penal camp.

After the meal the child began to doze. His father
made up a bed for him on the floor, tucked him up and
kissed him – and the boy declared that he had never
been more comfortable.

'I should like to try my new pipe. . . .'

'Well, why not? We'll open the window-pane and
there will be no smell.'

He filled the new English pipe that I had brought
him with good tobacco and began smoking with an
extraordinary sense of comfort.

'Remarkably good pipe, and tobacco, too. I'll make a
present to someone of my old one. I was much envied
for it, though I made it myself. But this one is a perfect
treasure. What is it called? Dunhill? A dream of a
pipe.' . . . A little ashamed of his naïve joy, he added,

thoughtfully: 'All these things – a pipe, slippers, food – belong to a world that is hopelessly closed to us. . . . It seems wonderful, for instance, to undress and get into bed. Strictly speaking, I haven't undressed for over a year.'

'But surely you did in prison?'

'How could I? In the common cell there were one hundred to one hundred and ten men to seventy square metres of space. We slept in two layers: one on the floor and another on a sort of plank bed over them. At *Kresty* they put four or six of us into cells meant for solitary confinement. There was nowhere to put one's things down – dirt, lice and bugs everywhere. The most one could do was to take off one's suit. And here one can't do even that. In the barracks we have to sleep on boards side by side; the allowance of space is eighteen inches per man, but the place is so crowded that one has to lie on one's side or we shouldn't all get in; there's no room to lie on one's back. There are a thousand men in a barrack. It's fearfully cold and draughty and snow blows in. The stoves are hardly ever lighted, and there are such quantities of bugs round them that one can't go near.'

'Do you all live like that?'

'Yes. No, not all,' he corrected himself with a smile. 'A "hostel for specialists" is just going to be opened in the town. The OGPU took a house, ordered plank beds for everyone, engaged a cook and a charwoman. The prisoners will be given special rations and will be able to wash and undress.'

'How many will live in the hostel?'

'There's room for thirty or forty.'

'Out of ten thousand prisoners?'

'There's only some eight thousand left now, the others have been sent to dig the canal.'

'I suppose the hostel will be for show?'

'Probably. Why, Gorki might arrive or Alexey Tolstoy, or some other writer or journalist. And in any case there will be an account of it in the official report. You know, at Solovki they made a film of the camp: prisoners had clothes given them for the occasion and were ordered to walk about and laugh.'

Our peaceful and happy mood vanished once more. We felt miserable again. All that I could bring and give was a drop in this ocean of hopeless suffering. Under a slight veil of hypocrisy the whole system was really meant to destroy the prisoners wholesale.

My husband sat there, pale and thoughtful.

'I have a mad idea,' he said, almost inaudibly, 'to escape. Do you remember how we used to talk of it before my arrest?'

'Yes.'

'Is it madness?'

'Perhaps it is, but it may be the only way.'

'I have thought it all out. Listen. Give me paper and pencil.' Silently and quickly he drew an exact map of the western shore of the White Sea – bays, coves, lakes, the river that flowed from the west, the railway line, several stations.

'In the summer you must come to see me here,' he said, pointing to the map. 'I shall do my best to get sent to that spot. If I say in a letter something about the south, it will mean that I have had no luck, but if I mention "north" it will mean that all is well. Or I may be sent to another place, there,' he said, pointing to the map again. 'In that case you will have to get out at the station before and walk some eight miles to meet me. You must both be ready and carry in your hold-alls all that's necessary.'

'How should we find the way?'

'It's a straight road beginning just beyond the station. The train arrives at night, but the nights will be light in the summer; it's beyond the Arctic circle.'

He told me exactly where we should have to meet.

'How shall I know the date?'

'In my letter I will mention a number, that will mean the date on which you must be on the spot. It must be in July, it's the driest month and there are berries and mushrooms then. But I think I'll contrive to be sent to this place here,' he pointed to the point he first indicated, 'and get permission for you to come and see me there. That will be much simpler, and then we can set out together. You'd better bring with you a razor to shave off my beard and a change of clothes for me. Everyone would know me with my black beard and in this leather coat. Shall we tell him?' he asked, looking at the boy, sound asleep in his corner.

'No, it would be too much for him. We'll tell him afterwards, on the way.'

'But perhaps it's madness?' my husband said, turning pale again.

'No, it's quite right. There is no other way. I can't bear to look on this senseless horror any more. Our lives have been ruined, the boy will be done for, too. We must escape while we can.'

'That's all I live by, this thought of escape. I believe that if all one's energies are directed to one purpose, one is bound to succeed.'

Now we talked freely and happily, discussing the details of our plan. We recalled the past, told each other of the sad fate of our friends, but our hearts were light because a new force was born in us, raising us above all that we had been through. We felt that we had found a way out and that a new, free and happy life lay before us.

I saw a great deal at Kem. I saw the camp, surrounded by barbed wire, with hideous wooden barracks and turrets on which sentries were posted; all around it there was a muddy swamp. I saw men from all parts of U.S.S.R. – Caucasians, Ukrainians, who sometimes were exiled together with their carts and oxen, Siberians, Tartars from the Volga, peasants from central Russia. I saw several professors, a great number of engineers and doctors. I saw a pitiable group of old priests, bent and white-haired, in torn cassocks belted with a string; they were made night-watchmen, and when all the other prisoners returned to the barracks, they hobbled along, leaning on their sticks, to watch over the property of the OGPU.

I saw an old cathedral, one of the most ancient in this part of the country; it was closed, and badly in need of repair. The parishioners had no longer the means to keep it up, and the Government did not care that the beautiful old building was perishing.

From the cathedral we walked to the churchyard. It had been snowing in the night and now everything was sparkling in the sunshine. The wooden crosses on the graves were painted in bright colours – blue, yellow, red, green – to take the place of flowers in that bare and wintry land. The peace of the past reigned in that churchyard. In those parts people lived to be seventy, eighty and ninety. They were strong and were in no hurry either to live or to die.

At the end of the churchyard we came across a huge open pit; stones and frozen lumps of earth lay round its sides, and it was filled to within three feet of the top.

'What is this?' I asked with instinctive horror.

'A grave,' my husband answered vaguely.

'Whose grave? So huge, and open?'

'The prisoners'. A common grave, so that it needn't be filled up each time. In winter the ground is frozen and is hard to dig and, besides, there wouldn't be room to bury them separately.'

We walked away, overcome once more with gloomy thoughts. A few feet from the churchyard we met a cart with four or five coffins placed in it. Several prisoners, blue with the cold, walked dejectedly behind it, carrying spades. They were followed by two soldiers with rifles.

.   .   .   .

On the evening of the following day we had to go home. My husband was allowed to see us off at the station – a rare favour, but a perfectly safe one: he could not very well escape with a family at the station full of OGPU officers.

It was dark at the station. We entered an unlighted, half-empty carriage. In another fifteen minutes we should be gone and he would return to the camp.

He was still standing beside me in the dark corridor. Fourteen minutes were left. The hand of the clock moved another minute – now it was thirteen.

I think that if I had had to die in thirteen minutes I should have found words to say good-bye; but when I had to return to what had once been our home and he

– to go behind barbed wire, I could not utter a syllable. Twelve minutes were left us.

I heard them tapping the wheels; water was brought into the carriages. A peasant woman with a baby and a bundle was trying to get into the train; the conductor rudely drove her away. Another minute passed. An OGPU officer standing under the lamp on the platform, scrutinised all the passers-by. Ten minutes. . . .

My husband was holding both my hands and saying something, but I did not hear, I could not take it in. Nine minutes. I could see nothing, tears flowed from my eyes like water. I could not control myself. How silly! Breaking down like that, at the last moment. . . .

'What is it, darling? What has happened?' I heard my husband's voice as in a dream.

'Nothing,' I just managed to say through my tears.

'This is the last time we part, we shall go away. . . .' All I understood was that the train was just going.

'Good-bye, daddy!' I heard the boy's voice full of tears.

'Good-bye! Good-bye till summer. We shall meet then and part no more.'

·

CHAPTER II

LEAVE-TAKING

I CAME back from the visit in a confused state of mind. And so, we were going away for good! This life was done with, and we did not know whether we should find our way to a new one. Our native land had given us our fill of sorrow – and yet it was our native land, whoever might be ruling it.   ·

Well, I had to get ready: to sell some things, to buy others, to think out what we should want. Top boots, sweaters, knapsacks, food. . . . He said that sugar and bacon were essential, because they were the most nourishing and compact. I must try and get some rice, prepare a few rusks. We should be a week or perhaps ten days on the way. We should want money. He asked me to bring two or three thousand roubles. Our notes were said to be of no value abroad, but we might have to hire a guide or to bribe someone on the way.

I began selling my possessions; I went to friends, to shops that took things on commission, to second-hand booksellers. I had to be careful not to attract attention, for the least trifle might cause the OGPU to exile me, and that would ruin everything.

It took me weeks to realise two or three hundred roubles, and I had to pay one hundred and fifty roubles for a pair of second-hand boots, one hundred roubles

for a sweater; I despaired of ever getting together all
that we needed.

I could not ask a single friend to help me because to
know or to suspect that someone contemplates escape
from U.S.S.R., and not to denounce him, is a crime
punishable by at least five years penal servitude. We
had to arrange everything unaided, being hardly able
to communicate with each other: once a month my
husband could send me a letter that passed through the
OGPU censorship, and I had to gather my directions
from symbolic words and signs we had agreed upon at
Kem.

I calmed down only a few days before our departure;
there was nothing more I could do, anyway.

I wanted to say good-bye to the Hermitage. I went
there like an ordinary visitor, paid at the entrance, and
walked round all my favourite halls. I could not help
noticing what was still in place and what had disappeared for ever.

Houdon's *Diana* was sold abroad; in the Italian
rooms there were so many losses that it made me feel
quite sad. Botticelli's *Adoration of the Kings* was sold –
the only Botticelli that we had in the Hermitage;
Rafael's lovely *Madonna Alba* was sold and so was
Titian's *Venus with the Mirror*. Less than a half, so far as
the best and authentic pictures are concerned, was left
of the once magnificent collection of Rembrandt. *Jan
Sobieski*, *Athene*, the portrait of Rembrandt's son, *The
Girl with the Broom*, the portrait of an old woman, had
all disappeared. The best pictures of the 'lesser Dutch-
men', Terburg and Metzu were gone also. Van Dyck's
Lord Wharton, Ruben's *Helen Furman* were missing, and
many, many other things. In the French rooms I

missed Watteau's *Mezzotint*; hardly anything was left of the beautiful collection of Germain's silver and the luxurious 'Orlov' service.

As I was about to go I met one of the young assistants. She sank on to a chair in utter exhaustion.

'I am sorry, I simply cannot stand. We are done to death with meetings, committees, plans, reports, and I haven't been able to have any dinner for two days. What were you doing here?'

'Looking at the remains of the Hermitage. I still love it, you know.'

'Perhaps one might love it if one didn't work in it,' she said sadly. 'It seems to me it is nothing but diagrams, schedules, classifications, Marxism. I think you are lucky to have left your post.'

'You mean, to have lost my post,' I corrected her.

.   .   .   .

There was so much to do before going away that I hardly noticed how the weeks passed. I felt as though I had not had time to look round before we found ourselves in the train, going along the route that we remembered only too well. We again saw prisoners digging by the railway, the wives going on a visit and shyly keeping apart from other passengers. But I no longer felt one of them – I was going not on a visit but much, much further, and from time to time a wave of gay recklessness came over me.

A group of students sent from the Forestries Institute to act as overseers on timber-works were travelling with us. They were not very cheerful about it. Only a few had been given top boots – the others would have to tramp about the forest in worn town shoes. None were provided with mosquito-nets. The supply of

food given them was barely enough for the journey –
and they rightly doubted whether they could buy
provisions on the spot. They could not refuse going
because it had been decided at the general meeting of
the Institute that the students were to be sent to timber-
works during the vacation.

I could not go to sleep; the northern night was light,
the carriage was hot and stuffy, sand and smuts were
blowing in at the open windows.

'Why aren't you asleep?' I heard one of the students
ask another.

'I was thinking of Mishka. He was murdered last
year, you remember?'

'Not in these parts.'

'But it was at timber-works, anyway.'

The others were arguing about the geography of the
parts where they were going; they knew nothing about
it. It was settled almost at the last moment which of
them were going to Karelia, which to the Urals or to
Siberia, so that they had not had time to read up the
subject. When I began answering their naïve, elemen-
tary questions, which I could have answered as a
schoolgirl, the whole group of them settled beside me
and listened as to a lecture.

'That's fine! A travelling university!' they said ap-
provingly, making notes, and asking more questions.
They were sorry I could not come with them: 'You
would teach us a thing or two.'

I very much wanted to tell them that in the part
where they were going there were several thousand
prisoners far better qualified than I; but this would
be 'counter-revolutionary propaganda', so I said
nothing.

My little boy was in the best of spirits, chattered and sang; he knew quite as many songs as the students.

Travelling in this fashion we arrived at the station where my husband was to meet us, as he said in his letter. We came out of the train, but could not see him anywhere. Could I have misunderstood him?

'There's daddy,' the boy whispered.

My husband was standing at the end of the train; he was obviously feeling very nervous. An OGPU official was standing between him and us.

What can it mean? I wondered. Hasn't he got the permit for our visit? or isn't he supposed to be at the station?

At that moment the OGPU official's attention was drawn to some men quarrelling on the platform; we hastily seized our things, walked round the train and reached some buildings behind which my husband joined us.

He was paler than before and looked quite ill.

'What's the matter with you?' I asked him almost before greeting him.

'Oh, it's nothing. I damaged my back a little. I had to lift a wet net weighing about three hundredweight. I slipped and fell on the hillside. When they lifted the net off my back I couldn't walk and had to crawl to my bunk.'

'When did it happen?' I asked, scrutinising him anxiously.

'Two or three days ago. I am up for the first time to-day. I haven't been able to lift my head. But I am much better to-day.'

Better, indeed! I thought gloomily. What would happen to us all?

'But everything has turned out splendidly: I have received permission for your visit and we have ten days to ourselves. I have hired a room for you with some peasants here, right by the sea. I am just going to take you there.'

He brought us to a boat and sat down to the oars. He rowed with difficulty and beads of perspiration came out on his face.

'I've grown very weak during these days,' he said apologetically. 'I couldn't get down any food to speak of.'

'And are you hungry now?'

'Yes,' he admitted shyly. 'But I can wait. No, no, don't bother just now,' he said, seeing that I picked up my bag.

But when I produced the remainder of the provisions we had for the journey he put down his oars and we all began eating as on a picnic.

It was only when he felt a little better that I noticed what a lovely place we were in.

The bay was broad and deep; the curved line of the shore was broken by numberless coves. Hills covered with pine forest rose all round; some of the crests could be seen beyond the line of the trees.

There was perfect stillness on the desolate beach. On one of the slopes a miserable tent could be seen.

'There are our prisoners, drying nets,' my husband said, pointing to it.

'Is that where you live?'

'Yes.'

'Does it leak?'

'Yes,' he answered unconcernedly. 'At first it was fearfully cold. We shivered like dogs and there was no shelter from the rain. But now the weather is drier and warmer.'

I knew that we should go away, but it was dreadful to think of these men, far beyond the Arctic circle, condemned to work in the sea and having nowhere to get warm or dry or to cook any food when it rained, because their tiny home-made stove stood under the open sky.

'Why, it's a wonderful piece of luck to be sent off to this sort of work,' said my husband with a smile, guessing my thoughts. 'Anyway, one isn't in the barracks and not behind barbed wire. Only fishermen have such good fortune.'

He brought us to a peasant cottage. It was much poorer than the one at Kem. There were no shining copper mugs and pans, no down pillows. The old man slept in the attic and the old woman and the grandchildren – their mother was dead – on the floor in the kitchen. Besides fish – if the old man succeeded in catching any – they had milk and butter from their cow. To feed it, the old woman and the eldest granddaughter brought every day branches from the forest; they preserved them for fodder in winter, and in the autumn they dried deer-moss. Almost all the meadows in the neighbourhood had been taken for the collective farm. Although the old people were also made to join, they never got anything from it: they were always told that they had not done enough work to secure a share of the produce.

Sugar was such a rarity that no one in the neighbourhood had set eyes on it for the last two or three years. There was no tea either. They heated the samovar and drank hot water with berries in it.

The old woman worked from morning till night. When I asked her when was she going to rest, she answered good-humouredly:

'I'll rest when I am dead. The summer is short in our parts; if one doesn't make provision in the summer, there will be nothing to eat in winter. There's branches to get for the cow, berries to pick and pickle, then there will be mushrooms to salt and to dry. It's not like the old times – you can't buy flour when you want it. No pie-baking nowadays. You just have your ration and live on it as best you can.'

It was the same story everywhere. Life has been reduced to a mere struggle for existence.

Every morning my husband went to do his work and did not come back to us till the evening. All day long he was watched by the OGPU escort and by his fellow prisoners, who might give him away any moment if they noticed anything suspicious. But at night we were free and could go from the cottage to the neighbouring forest. There was a clearing there made by a forest fire. One could see a long way from there and could not be overheard.

'We'll soon be out of this,' my husband said. 'We must choose a day when I am not supposed to go to work. Then it will be a good twenty hours before I am missed.'

'You know, I still don't understand how it is that we've been allowed to come and see you here.'

'Ah, it was my marine zoology that did the trick!' my husband laughed. 'You remember what it was like at Kem? Sentries all over the place, two hundred miles to the frontier, swamps all round and, besides, one would be missed within a few hours. OGPU knows very well that no one can escape from there, especially with a family. It took some planning to get away from the camp. . . . First of all, I had to convince them that I did not mean to escape and at the same time to invent all sorts of reasons for being sent to different places. I invented a new way of killing salmon and a year ago they sent me to teach it to the fishermen. Salmon is exported to England and I earned them a good many English pounds by that. Another time they sent me to investigate all their Fisheries, and my report was of such practical as well as scientific value that even they could not fail to see it. It never occurred to them, of course, that at the same time I looked out a suitable place for our escape. As a reward I was allowed to see you at Kem, but after that was again shut up behind barbed wire all the winter. In the spring I was transferred to Soroka and that was worse than ever. I nearly went mad there. Then I made a discovery which in any other country would have made me a rich man. I found a way of utilising stickleback. It's a fish about nine centimetres long, with bristles on its back, on its belly, on the front fins. It's a voracious little creature and devours other fishes' spawn, and is a nuisance, too, because it gets in between the meshes of the net. Well, I made an experiment – with nothing but a primus and a saucepan at my disposal – and obtained from it good oil and fish-meal admirably suited for fodder. Considering our acute shortage of fats and of fodder, it really was an important discovery. And this is what saved us. I have been sent to this place because the best catches of stickleback are here and, as a reward, was allowed to see you on the spot so that I need not interrupt my work. The chief of the camp himself signed my pass, convinced that I have put untold riches into their hands. It's perfectly true that if they follow it up, the results will be of enormous value to the country. I have paid them liberally for my ten days without armed escort at my back all the time. But I am not going to work for them any more. Now we must escape – there won't be another such opportunity.'

·

CHAPTER III

It had rained the whole day before but towards evening the wind changed and the sky cleared. The villagers were preparing to go fishing or haymaking at dawn.

'If we don't get off to-morrow, all is lost,' said my husband. 'In another two days your permit expires and you will have to go home. I'll never get sent to a place as good as this again.'

'Very well, let us set off to-morrow.'

'I'll go to our headquarters to-day and give in a report of my work – they like that – and also remind them that to-morrow is my off-day. Then they won't miss me till the day after.'

When he went away, taking the boy with him, I looked for the tenth time over our things. I simply could not get the most essential ones packed into three knapsacks. Sugar and bacon took up a lot of room, and we had to take some rice and a few rusks as well. And we had to have a change of underclothes and something warm, too.

Late in the evening when the boy was asleep my husband and I sorted everything out for the last time.

'We must have a change of leg-wrappers for each one of us.' I tore up two sheets for the purpose – and our knapsacks grew still more bulky.

226

'Have you made waterproof bags for matches, salt and sugar?'

I sat down to make them there and then, pricking my fingers – I was never any good at sewing.

We went on packing and repacking till late at night. I grew quite dizzy, and my husband's back began to ache, so we had to go to bed without finishing our job.

I could not go to sleep till daybreak and then it was time to get up. The boy ran to wash himself at the bay.

'We must make haste and finish packing,' my husband hurried me. 'When shall we tell the boy?'

'On the way.'

'He'll wonder why we are taking the knapsacks.'

'I'll tell him we are going for a picnic and will sleep out. I'll tell our landlady the same.'

I saw that my husband was looking at me in alarm. 'What's the matter?'

'Your dress! It's light blue, it can be seen a mile off!'

'I haven't got another.'

'That's dreadful. . . . We ought to have thought of that.'

'I'll put on my brown overall.'

I had just pinned the overall to the window by way of a curtain so that the neighbours should not see that we had gone.

We sat down to breakfast but were too excited to eat.

When we had finished and the boy had gone to get the boat ready, my husband stopped me:

'We can't leave the place so untidy – it gives the show away.'

We washed up and tidied the room. We kept getting in each other's way, unable to master our agitation.

'How much longer will you be?' said the boy coming

in. 'All the villagers have gone. Shall I take the sail, daddy?'

'Yes, do. We are just coming. Take this knapsack. Is it heavy?'

'No. Not if I don't have to carry it far.'

He went out. We exchanged glances. How would the boy manage on the journey with that knapsack?

'Have you taken the xeroform?'

'No.'

'Where is it?'

'I don't know.'

We began searching for it. The xeroform had disappeared as though by magic.

'Have we any other disinfectant?'

'No.'

My husband was in despair. We could not find it. Afterwards, on the journey, we remembered that it was in the pocket of the overcoat which we had decided not to take with us.

'Where is the compass?'

'I brought it here and put it on the table.'

'It isn't there.'

Superstitious fear possessed me. I knew I had brought the compass into the room. It was not on the table, not on the window-sills. We had had an awful time with that compass already. A prisoner, found in possession of a compass, is shot, because a compass is regarded as certain proof of his planning to escape. My husband had given his compass to me to hide. When a prisoner's relatives come on a visit, the OGPU often makes a search in their lodgings to make sure that they had not brought with them anything forbidden. I wrapped the compass in paper and hid it among the

onions in a sieve in the larder. Our landlady wanted
the sieve one day and turned out the onions on the
floor. I nearly went off my head looking for my tiny
paper parcel in that larder. I found it at last under a
potato bag, and now it was lost again.

Mechanically I picked up my husband's cap – and
there was the compass. He gave it to me again. He,
poor man, believed that I was his guide to safety,
and really I was a dead weight dragging us all
down.

I had no pocket; I wore a peasant kerchief over my
head so that my hat would not attract attention. I tied
the compass and the map into the corner of my kerchief.

What evil spirit prompted me to do that!

Now everything was ready and we had to leave our
last shelter.

My husband took me by the hands and kissed me.
We were both excited and happy – we were just going
to take the first step towards our new life.

We left the room, carefully shutting the door behind
us. The village was deserted; only tiny children were
playing in the road and an old man sat outside his
cottage.

'At last!' our son met us reproachfully. 'It's one
o'clock. The wind is changing. Where shall we go?'

'Straight on, down the bay.'

'It's a head wind, we can't put up the sail.'

'We'll row; perhaps it will be better when we get
beyond those rocks over there.'

We pushed off. The boy took the rudder oar. His
father had been teaching him to use it, but he was still
very bad at it.

We had to go against the wind and the tide, and our boat moved slowly.

The boy was in excellent spirits, fidgeted about and talked incessantly. My husband felt unhappy and irritable.

What was I to do? If I told the boy that this was not a picnic he would be upset, and it would be difficult in the boat to soothe and comfort him. It would mean more loss of time.

I changed places with the boy. I managed the rudder oar still worse, and he and my husband were continually correcting me. I suffered in silence but at last I tossed my head in exasperation and – I saw the compass and the map slowly sink into the deep water. On my shoulder lay the empty corner of my kerchief that had come undone.

'What?' said my husband, not daring to believe his eyes.

'The compass . . . and the map,' I answered, choking.

'Well, it's Fate,' said he, looking at me sadly and kindly.

'Why do you take on so, mother? It doesn't matter, we can buy another when we come home and send it to daddy,' the boy said naïvely.

I could not answer. I felt very bad. I gave the rudder to my son and sat down at the bottom of the boat. My head reeled, and I kept seeing the greenish water and the little metal box sinking into the depths. All that had seemed so simple – the bee-line to the West and Finland at the end of it, had now sunk into the depths, too. Should we return? We had not been missed yet. But to buy another compass I should have to go to Leningrad – a journey of almost forty-eight hours each

way. It was out of the question. If I could have sunk
into the green water together with the compass to save
the other two, I would have done it gladly! But it was
silly to think of it; one can't make bargains with
Fate.

'We shall have to struggle for another two hours if the
wind does not drop,' my husband said.

He had been rowing for four hours already. His
hands were blistered and one blister burst, showing
raw flesh. His heart was evidently feeling the strain, he
was getting breathless. I took his place for a time but
I was not much use.

At the last projection of the shore we stopped to take
breath and to see if there was anyone at the end of the
bay where our real escape was to begin. There seemed
to be nobody there. The wind had dropped. Evening
was coming on.

The boy stepped out of the boat and amused himself
sprinkling water on dragon-flies settled on the reeds by
the shore. 'You poor, poor child!' I thought. 'We don't
know if we'll bring you out of this alive and here you
are playing with dragon-flies.'

'What shall we do?' my husband asked me quietly.
'Perhaps we'd better go back?'

'You decide. If you think we can go without a compass and a map, I am ready.'

'If it keeps fine, I shall find the direction by the sun.
We shall get to Finland right enough, though it may
take us a day or two longer.'

'Then let us go.'

Rowing was easier now. Suddenly we heard loud
human voices. It was the haymakers making a fire and
settling for the night. Seeing our boat they called us to

join them, or perhaps simply exchanged remarks about us.

We sharply turned into another cove which appeared empty, but at the very end of it we saw the black silhouette of a fisherman. He was fixing his net, moving about leisurely.

The question was, what line would these people take? Our only hope was that it would not occur to them that we were runaways: no one had yet attempted to escape with a wife and a child.

We waited among the reeds. The fisherman finished his job and went away, and the others did not trouble themselves about us.

Then my husband rowed us up to a footpath and left there the basket with the remains of food and the sail, making it look as though it had been hidden. Then he rowed us to· the mouth of a stream. We stepped out of the boat.

'Wait for me here; I'll dispose of the boat and come back.' He took the boat some distance and tied it up carefully so that it would not look abandoned. It would have been better to sink it, but it is not an easy thing to do with a big sea-boat.

It was about nine in the evening. The sun had set behind the hills and the crests shone like gold. The forest looked one dark mass. The bay was smooth and still. The boy grew silent; he was sleepy and was probably beginning to feel that something was amiss.

My husband came back so noiselessly that we only saw him when he stood beside us.

'Fetch me some water, dear.' He drank greedily. 'Now, let us go, we must clear out of here as soon as possible.'

We put on our knapsacks and walked along an indistinct path blocked by fallen branches and trees. I had no time to think of anything: the knapsack weighed me down, I kept stumbling against the branches, I was gasping for breath and my one concern was not to fall or to lag behind. The air in the forest was moist and hot. My cheeks were burning, my mouth was dry, I desperately wanted a drink. Should we have to walk like this all the way? How would the boy stand it? He was walking well and apparently without difficulty: his father had been training him during these days. If only I did not let them down!

We walked like that for about an hour. The forest was plunged into an even twilight; there was no real darkness.

'Let us rest here and have a drink,' said my husband cheerfully but almost in a whisper.

'And where shall we put up for the night?' asked the boy, whispering like his father.

'Darling, we shall not put up for the night at all,' I said. 'We are going to Finland, escaping from U.S.S.R.'

The boy looked at me and, quite overcome, hid his face on his father's shoulder.

'Poor darling daddy. . . .'

His father kissed and petted him.

'You'll have a hard time of it, dear; the journey will be very difficult, but if we escape we shall be free people, there will be no OGPU.'

The boy did not know what to say: it was night, we were in a wild forest, we could not return home, we had to go into a strange country. . . . But he understood that it was for his father's sake.

'Let's go,' he said.

When we got up from the mossy ground I threw back the veil that I wore instead of a mosquito net. I wanted to have a drink and dab my face with water. Both my husband and my son suddenly stared at me with an expression of utter despair.

'What's the matter?' I asked in alarm.

'Your face is all puffy and swollen. How does your heart feel? Good heavens, what shall we do!'

'Mother, darling, what has happened to you?' the boy whispered, stroking my hands.

'Nothing special. You are absurd, you two. Put on your knapsacks and let's go.'

'No, you must take off your knapsack.'

'Mother, take it off, give it to daddy,' whispered the boy, almost in tears.

I sorrowfully took off my knapsack; my husband slung it on, along with his own. It was a fearful weight and I do not know that his heart was any stronger than mine, but the joy of freedom, the sympathy of the boy made everything easy to him. When we stopped to rest again, he told the boy all about our plans.

'This night we must walk as far as ever we can. We may be missed to-morrow: the haymakers saw us, and we shall not have returned to our lodgings. They'll let the OGPU know. It's just possible that they won't be ready to go after us at once, but they have a cutter and can get across the bay in an hour or two. This path goes to the timber-works, about twenty or twenty-five miles from here. As soon as we get past them, we'll turn towards the mountains and there they won't find us.'

'Daddy, is it far to Finland?'

'Yes, darling, it is. About seventy miles as the crow

flies, and we may have to walk a good hundred. And when we get there we may have to walk for several days before we find any people. But that won't matter, so long as we have crossed the frontier.'

We walked on again, and in the midnight darkness lost the path which we still needed, because it saved us time. The boy was frightened, and when his father went off to look for it, he began to complain that he felt ill and could not walk any further.

'Lie down and cover yourself up with your coat, head and all, so that the gnats don't bite you. We cannot go back because your father and I would be shot. Go to sleep.'

He curled himself up on the ground and went to sleep. That was his only moment of weakness; and after all, it was quite natural that he should want to be at home and sleep in his bed instead of walking through the damp, gloomy forest. We never heard another complaint from him.

My husband found the path and we went on. When dawn appeared behind the hills, the forest, ravines and swamps seemed less terrifying. We came upon some buildings, decided that they were the timber-works depot, and having left them behind, resolved to have a little sleep by a fallen pine tree.

'Take off your boots and hang up your leg-wrappers to dry. The chief thing is to keep our feet in good condition,' my husband instructed me.

The child dropped asleep blissfully. I could not go to sleep because of my heart, but a drowsiness stole over me. I vaguely felt that the sun was beginning to be warm, but suddenly big drops of rain fell upon me. I had to wake my husband and hastily retrieve our boots and leg-wrappers. The boy slept while pulling on his boots; I tried to push him awake, but he put his head in my lap and went to sleep again. He was warm all over though he lay on the bare ground.

'The path goes further west, the rain will soon stop; we must hurry on,' said my husband, who had been reconnoitring. 'Make haste; it's five o'clock. We've lost two hours here.'

We set off at a quick pace. We thought that we had passed the timber-works depot and that the path led only to the cutting in the forest.

It was a lovely part. In the depths of the valley flowed a fine river, now narrow and rapid like a mountain stream and now calm and wide. High fir trees grew on the steep banks. There was a perfect stillness. It was too late in the season for the birds to sing; we did not see any wild animals. My husband walked ahead, the boy followed him, and I came last; we kept at some distance from each other so as to be less easily seen.

I had not yet noticed anything suspicious when I suddenly saw my husband bend and, as it were, roll down a steep slope; the boy and I did the same.

Over the edge of the slope I saw that there were two or three houses in front of us. At the other bank of the river there was another house. There did not seem to be anyone about.

Panic-stricken we dashed into the forest, crossed a marsh and went up a hill. I lost all sense of direction. My veil was torn in several places, gnats got under it and were devouring my ears and blinding my eyes. Two mackintoshes and a coat rolled up into a bundle which I carried on my back came undone, and I had to take them on my arm. The sun was burning, and there was a moist heat in the forest. I was gasping for breath, and could not catch up with my husband and son: they evidently saw something and ran bending to the ground, going uphill all the way. At last they sat down behind a huge pine tree that had fallen on the ground; they were completely shielded by it. They were going to rest and have something to eat. I could not bear the thought of food; a vein was throbbing in my throat and all I wanted was to lie down. I threw myself on the ground within a few feet of them, covering my head with an overcoat to have a respite from mosquitoes. Hundreds of them had got into my hair, and the lobes of my ears were bleeding with the bites. I did not know how I could readjust my hat and veil while a yellow buzzing cloud of these monsters was hovering over me.

A few minutes passed. My heart was beginning to beat more evenly when I heard the clear sound of an axe quite near. I sat up, forgetting about the mosquitoes. My son, who was lying behind the pine tree, waved to me angrily. My husband crawled to the other side of the tree in the direction of the sound. It appeared that we had settled within some twenty-five yards of a house that was hidden by the trees. I hurriedly pulled on my hat, wrapped up my head with the veil, snatched up the coats in a bundle, and we dashed across a clearing covered with dazzling white deer-moss. Our one thought was to hide, for if we were seen it might be the end of us. Everyone here carried a rifle or an axe and we had nothing. We could not defend ourselves against two or three men and would be caught in no time. It would pay them well to give us up to the OGPU and they would not hesitate to do it.

We ran so long as we had any strength left. At last my husband took us to a pine tree on a steep slope and told us to lie down and rest while he went to scout.

'There are people all round,' he said when he came back. 'There's a lake and a house over there; I heard voices. We must clear out of here as soon as possible. This must be the timber-works headquarters.'

Barely stopping to take breath, he led us on. We went through copses that looked like a park, past a lake with white water-lilies, went down into ravines, climbed hills – I could make nothing of it. It seemed to me that we were circling round and round and would find ourselves in the same place again. But no – he took us to the slope of a hill and said firmly: 'The west is over there.' It might be, for aught I knew; I was quite sure that left to myself I could never have found either the west or the east and should have perished there, devoured by mosquitoes.

I do not know how far we had walked that day, but we had to stop early, because both the boy and I were completely exhausted. His father found for us a huge fir tree with fluffy branches that almost reached the ground. It was dry underneath, on the thick layer of fallen pine needles. The boy snuggled under his over-coat and dropped sound asleep.

We left our shelter at daybreak. The scenery was beautiful; there was no path and the forest looked quite deserted. We walked on happily, glad that we no longer felt like hunted beasts – and we came straight upon a clearing and a house! Again we had to run, crouching, and hide in the depths of the forest.

CHAPTER IV

ON THE WAY

WE left behind at last all traces of human habitation. There was virgin forest all round us. When we sat down to rest, choosing some fairly high spot in the wind where there were fewer mosquitoes, flocks of birds gathered around us, watching us with interest.

We were well aware that it was the third day of our escape, and that they were hunting for us high and low, and yet we could not help fancying at times that we were on a lovely picnic. We actually ventured to boil a kettle and have some tea – for the first time. My husband looked happier than I had seen him for years. He seemed younger and was full of vigour and confidence.

Towards evening the hills grew steeper and more wild. A curious white mist gathered around us. We could see nothing in the distance and constantly stumbled upon rocks or huge blocks of granite. Utterly worn out we climbed at last on to a plateau where a few trees twisted out of shape by the wind were dotted about.

'It's not much of a place. When it is light one can see right through it.'

'We'll move on at daybreak.'

'There's no water here.'

'I am not thirsty, and the boy is dropping with fatigue.'

'Very well, lie down and I'll go and look for water.'

Restless creature! He was so excited at being free that he was ready to walk night and day till he left behind the land where he had been a slave and a convict. But he had us two on his hands. The boy was so tired that he dropped fast asleep before I had had time to pull off his boots. I was as tired as he, but the moment I lay down I had the horrible thought that my husband might not find us! I jumped up and walked two or three paces away from our tree – I could see nothing. Then I came out on to the most open part of the plateau and decided to stand there till he came back. Minutes passed. It was damp and cold, I badly wanted to sit down, but he might miss me then. However much I strained my eyes I could see nothing but the fantastic distorted silhouettes of the trees.

At last what looked like one of these silhouettes moved up towards me.

'Where is the boy? I could hardly find our place.'

'Asleep under the pine tree.'

'Which one?'

'That one, over there. . . . No, more to the left. . . . No, I don't know which.'

Now my son was lost!

'Stand here so that I can have a landmark and I'll go and look for him,' said my husband.

He soon came back saying: 'I've found him.'

There was no doubt that he still had plenty of the primitive instincts of a huntsman: he had no difficulty in picking his way in the dark forest, while I felt utterly lost and helpless.

What a pitiable sight it was: two windblown pines

and under them three small lumps – two knapsacks
and a child huddled under a coat!

We went to sleep too, but presently my husband got
up and made some semolina porridge. We were not
hungry, though it was our first hot meal during the
three days. Big yellow mosquitoes kept dropping into
the spoons. The boy was too sleepy to open his mouth
properly, though we put plenty of sugar on his semolina. We all felt very tired.

We set off in the same direction as before, but soon
found that we were going further away from the
valley and the hills were getting higher and higher.

'We must go down to the river,' said I. 'We are losing
the main valley.'

'Why, how can we go to the path where they may
be stalking us at this very minute?' my husband
protested.

We walked on.

'I am sure something is leading us astray. I wonder if
that river has a tributary?' I persisted.

My husband gave in. We decided to go down and
see in what direction the river was flowing. The lower
we descended, the thicker was the undergrowth; our
way was continually blocked by dead trees with sharp,
prominent branches; it was very marshy underfoot.
Our feet were wet through, our hands scratched, our
clothes torn, but it was worth while: we found that a
tributary of the river the course of which we were
following really did take us away from the main
valley. That tributary was not marked on the map,
which we had studied carefully and still remembered.
It was essential for us to cross it, and it was wide, rapid
and deep. Fortunately it divided into several streams

near the junction with the bigger river. The rich meadow land all round was overgrown with white umbelliferous flowers and bright pink mullen. My husband went to look for a ford, and we rested. The air was warm and fragrant, and if it had not been for thick clouds of mosquitoes, the morning would have been quite perfect.

What a beautiful part of the country it was, and how full of promise! All this was virgin soil, almost unknown to man. How much work and energy is needed to utilise Russia's enormous resources, and yet her best workers are exiled to penal camps and killed off by the thousand. The OGPU, which has appropriated all this region, does nothing but devastate it, destroying the forests, which will take hundreds of years to grow.

We began the crossing: my husband found two small trees that had fallen into the water almost opposite each other, and led across first me, then the boy, and then carried one by one our knapsacks. Our bridge was rickety and threatened to give way under us; at the opposite bank we had to step on to a partially submerged old stump, wet and slippery. The crossing took us over an hour. My husband became exhausted and hungry, and his clothes were wet. It was annoying to lose so much time when we could already see the end of the main valley before us. The rest of the way seemed easy: the bank of the bigger river that flowed from the west was flat and overgrown with branching elm trees; the mountains on the horizon did not seem very steep. A lovely smooth path made by the deer ran along the edge of the water.

'No, that won't do,' my husband said decisively.

'The path is so good that men may use it as well as deer. If the OGPU have a grain of sense they won't hunt for us in the mountains, but will waylay us here. No, my dears, we must get back to the hills.'

We began climbing up the sunlit, sparsely wooded slope where we could still be seen.

'I wonder if we'd better have a rest,' my husband said irresolutely. 'I am tired out with that crossing.'

'Excellent. Let us have a rest. We'll walk all the better afterwards.'

We sat down behind a huge fir-tree that hid us from the valley. The father and the son went to sleep. I sat and sewed. I had to make myself a proper mosquito-net because my ears were one sore; the boy's mosquito-net wanted mending. I had no material to patch it up with and had to tear the hem of my apron for the purpose. This was the best rest we were having since we started. My husband had not had more than four hours sleep during the three days.

I was sorry to wake them, but there was nothing for it. Clouds were gathering and we had to hurry. Our feet were swollen with constant walking, and it was perfect agony to pull on our boots, stiff after drying in the sun. The boy had a blister on his heel, and we had no disinfectant of any kind. I only hoped it would not fester.

We went on again, climbing hills and descending into ravines. The slope on the opposite bank of the river was very picturesque. It was all covered with white deer moss, with small fir-trees dotted about here and there.

'What a jolly place for hunting!' my husband exclaimed thoughtlessly. 'Especially on horseback.'

'Unfortunately, just now we are the hunted and not the hunters.'

'Yes, we'd better not go down there till dusk,' he answered sadly.

The bank on this side was growing steeper and more rocky, and between the stones it was a wet bog. Towards sunset we reached a point where the river turned sharply to the north.

'We must not follow the river course any longer, but walk on towards the west and cut across the ridge over there, where that depression is. We'll have to wait for dusk to cross the river,' said my husband anxiously.

We chose a secluded spot and sat down. The boy wrapped himself up in his coat, head and all, and immediately went to sleep. He developed a happy faculty of dropping asleep every time we stopped to rest, and it was this that saved him. He was not really very strong and his heart was troublesome from his early childhood.

We roused him when the sun had set and a white mist began to rise from the ground. We were going to descend to the river, but it was not a simple matter. We had to go down what looked a sheer wall of rock. We tried to find a better place, but it was the same everywhere. The sun had set, darkness was coming on, thick mist was rising in the valley, and we could not waste any time. We had at all costs to cross the river that night so as to walk through the dangerous open ground on the other side before daybreak.

It was only from sheer despair that one could attempt such a descent. Sometimes we picked our way along projections in the rock where there was scarcely room to put one's foot, sometimes we rolled down in

the hope of catching hold of a bush on the way – and
the bush, instead of being a support, slid down with us.
We had to lower our knapsacks, too, which we could
not carry on our backs.

The boy was wonderful. He was very sleepy and
probably considered that it was no use thinking about
danger when father and mother were with him and
no doubt knew where they were leading him. And so
he quite readily rolled down the slope towards his
father, who caught him in his arms and sent him on
further, in front of or behind the knapsacks. When at
last we found ourselves at the bottom and looked back
on our course, I made haste to turn away so as not to
think of it. I do not know how it was that we did not
break our arms and legs.

Crossing the river in the mist and darkness is also
a thing I don't care to recall. The river was wider and
swifter than the one we had crossed in the morning.
It would have been impossible to wade through it in
the cold night, amidst clouds of mosquitoes. We had
to cross by walking on the thick branches and whole
trees that had fallen into the river, but the first one
we stepped on broke down under my husband's weight,
and he had some difficulty in getting out of the water.
The rest, too, were very unsteady, and we had to walk
on them in turn, while the dark water of the mountain
river roared and foamed underneath.

But we had no choice in the matter. Our one dream
was to find a dry spot and go to sleep.

·

CHAPTER V

A NIGHT IN THE SWAMP

IT was an unpleasant night. The only dry spot we could find was by the roots of a huge fir-tree. We had to lie there doubled up because it was hopelessly wet all round. The hard grey moss soaked with the rain and the mist was like a sponge full of water. The air was full of tiny drops of moisture and thick with buzzing mosquitoes. A dense mist covered the tall fir-trees from top to bottom.

Our boots, leg-wrappings and socks were wet through; we had to take them off and wrap our feet in dry rags. Mosquitoes were so dreadful that we had to wind round our necks and arms everything we possessed – stockings, pants, shirts. After the hot, tiring day, the damp and cold of the Arctic marsh penetrated us right through.

The boy slept pressed close to me and managed to get warm. My husband dozed off, but woke up every minute with a groan. I simply could not go to sleep. My whole body felt cold and stiff; I wanted to stretch my legs, but that meant putting my feet into water. The night seemed endless.

As soon as the mist began to lift, I woke up my husband. He was shivering with the cold and could not stop his teeth from chattering. It was only three in the morning. I was sorry to wake the boy, who was sound asleep, but we had to make haste and go away from the slope where our dark figures could be seen miles away against the background of white moss.

I was afraid that the boy would be shivering like his father, but no, he woke up rosy and cheerful as though he had been sleeping in bed.

'What are you doing?' he asked sleepily.

'Time to go. Put on your boots.'

'I am sleepy.'

'When we come to a dry place you can have another sleep. We must cross the slope before the sun gets to it.'

He obediently began pulling on his damp boots.

'Does your heel hurt? Let me have a look.'

He angrily waved me away. It certainly was no joke baring his foot with clouds of bloodthirsty mosquitoes hovering over us.

As we walked the moss squelched underfoot like a wet sponge; cold water got inside our boots. But we felt warmer walking, and anyway it was better than sitting in the swamp.

The ground rose steeply, but as far as the eye could see it was one continuous expanse of white moss with its tiny, orange-coloured tubular flowers and here and there the reddish caps of the 'aspen' fungi. It was strange to see the familiar Russian fungi among the white moss, rocks and granite.

The clouds that had completely covered the sky began to part, and a narrow orange strip of the dawn appeared beyond the mountains. It was growing dangerously light, and we suddenly came upon several paths running parallel to one another. There were no human footprints on them, but no trace of deer either. Carefully stepping across so as not to leave a footmark we rushed in alarm higher up the incline.

The frontier might be near and these paths might have been made by the frontier-guards. Every moment we expected to see a horseman in khaki uniform with green stripes. He could easily catch us all – there was nowhere to hide.

Breathless with the steep climb we walked on without stopping to rest or looking back.

'Perhaps they are deer paths?' I whispered to my husband.

'There are no hoof marks. And why do they run from north to south?'

We had just begun walking in a more leisurely way when we came upon another set of paths going in the same direction as the first. Again we rushed uphill almost at a run.

We were desperately thirsty. The moss underfoot was so wet that one could wring it out, but there was not a single stream or pool. Occasionally we saw some cranberries, but they were still unripe – white and bitter.

We walked for one hour, for two hours, we came to some huge blocks of granite with small, twisted birch-trees and willows growing in the crevices, and yet the top of the crest seemed as far off as ever.

The sun had risen. In the rarified transparent air its light seemed keen and cold. In the distance, beyond the thin layers of cloud, we caught glimpses of dark mountain ridges with a hard, menacing outline.

When I learned geography at school I imagined that the Arctic North was one flat, continuous, frozen marsh. But what we now saw before us might have been Switzerland, except that there the mountains part occasionally, showing the calm blue surface of lakes, while here the black, rocky peaks seemed piled on the top of one another as though on purpose to prevent anyone from trying to scale their desolate waste.

.

·

CHAPTER VI

'SOFT STONE'

A T last we came upon a hollow surrounded by enormous blocks of bare granite. There was a tiny lake at the bottom. The water in it looked black and still, and next to it lay a piece of granite flat as a table.

'I can no more,' I cried. I felt so weak that I could not stand. I threw myself on the granite, covering my head with the mackintosh through which the mosquitoes could not sting.

I lost consciousness instantly and dreamt that I had sunk into the still, dark water of the lake.

I was awakened by a whisper close by. The father and the son were getting tea ready. There was hot water in the kettle, a mug did the duty of a teapot, lumps of bacon were placed on the rusks. Sugar could not be put out, because mosquitoes would settle on it immediately, though there were much fewer of them here than down in the marsh. This was the second time in the four days that we had tea. It tasted incredibly good, and revived us wonderfully.

The sun stood high, the sky was clear and blue. We felt as safe in our hollow as in an impregnable fortress. Now that we were out of the dangerous valley it seemed impossible for our pursuers to detect us. *We had escaped*. It was a delightful moment of rest.

'Mother, your stone must be very soft?' the boy teased me.

'Lovely and soft. I don't think I ever slept so soundly.'

We talked in whispers about the Alps, the Andes, the Himalayas, about anything that came into our heads. The world was opening before us, and a free and happy life seemed within our reach.

We were looking for the last time at the black ridges of mountains going East, towards the sea which we had left behind. Heavy storm clouds lay over it, while here the sun was shining brightly. We counted the peaks that we had passed, proud that there were so many of them, but the boy seemed rather uneasy: he understood only now how far we had gone from all the places he knew.

'Look at U.S.S.R. It may be for the last time!'

He looked, as though not quite believing that over there was his native land, which he was leaving for ever; or perhaps he did believe it, and was sad. His home, his comrades, all that he knew and loved was there. If it had not been for the terrible and mysterious prison where both his father and mother had disappeared in turn, he would have been leaving behind a happy childhood, with all its dreams and hopes.

My heart was aching too and it was bitter to me to say good-bye to my unhappy country. I loved Russia, sincerely and devotedly, loved her through all the misery, fear and bewilderment to which she had been reduced. I had worked for my people without sparing myself, but we had been deprived of all that makes life worth living – freedom and the work we loved. There was no other way for us.

We had now to leave behind the last Russian river and go across unknown hills. Should we come alive out of this labyrinth of mountain ridges, without a map or a compass? Should we find our way to Finland? Or were we still on this side of the frontier and might be shot at any moment? Danger was ahead and all round us, and yet I knew that if by some magic I had been brought home once more, I should have made the same choice over again.

CHAPTER VII

SQUIRREL'S HOUSE

AFTER resting we walked straight, as we thought, in the direction of the frontier. It was somewhere on the other side of the ridge, but we did not know how far it was. Walking was easy now there was grass and not wet moss underfoot. The trees – birches and firs – were beautiful as in a park; the firs were big and shapely, the birches small, with twisted branches, curiously like apple trees. It was warm, a light breeze was blowing and mosquitoes did not pester us. The bare, rocky ridge in front stood out so sharply against the sky that we could not help wondering whether it was the actual frontier.

Suddenly the boy began to lag behind.

'What is it?' I saw that something was wrong.

'It's all right. Go on, I'll walk behind.'

But, turning round suddenly, I found that he was dragging one foot and leaning heavily on his stick.

'Why are you limping?'

'I knocked my foot, it will be all right in a minute.'

'Does your boot hurt you?'

'No, go on,' he answered irritably. He was obviously doing his best, understanding how fatal the slightest delay might be, but the pain and the effort of walking made his face look pale and drawn. We went on so

long as he could walk, but at last we had to stop and
see what was the matter.

We stopped by two magnificent fir-trees. Their
branches spread widely over the ground and the earth
underneath, covered with dry needles, was soft and
warm. Breaking off the small dry branches inside we
crawled under the branches and hid there as in a tent.
The boy lay down, we took off his boot, unwrapped his
sore foot, and went cold with horror: there was a huge,
ugly-looking abscess on his heel. How could the child
have walked at all!

We said nothing; the boy looked questioningly at us,
and we at each other.

'Whatever shall we do, my poor, poor boy!' said his
father in despair.

'I don't know, daddy,' he answered so sweetly that I
felt like crying.

'We must open it,' I said.

'But how can we, when we have no disinfectant?'

'We can disinfect the razor in the fire. Water here is
pure.' I took a roll of bandages out of the knapsack.
Another piece of bad luck – they had got wet in the
marsh during the night. They would have to be washed
in a stream and dried in the sun, in the hope that
everything must be pure at such an altitude. My husband went to look for water and we remained lying
under the fir-tree.

'Mother, are you sure we can't be seen here at
all?'

'Quite sure. One can't see under this fir within five
paces of it, and it is exactly like other fir-trees – they
could not search each one.'

'And if they had a dog with them?'

'A dog follows scent. It could not track us all the way from the valley in that wet moss.'

'And what if they came from the frontier?'

'But there would be no footprints to guide them.'

'Mother, do you remember, in the theatre, when we went to see *Uncle Tom's Cabin*, what a dreadful dog there was? It caught the negress who wanted to escape with her baby to the Free States.'

'You mustn't think of it, darling, no one will find us here. It was dangerous down in the valley, but now they can't possibly guess where we have gone.' I spoke calmly and persuasively, though my very soul was trembling with fear.

My husband came back, pale and anxious. He knew better than we did how desperate our situation was.

'I can't cut it, my hands are shaking,' he said, when he prepared the razor.

I volunteered, but set about it so clumsily that I might have made matters worse.

'You'd better cut it, daddy! Don't be afraid, I'll be all right. Only tell me when you are going to begin.'

He made ready, clutched my hand and said:

'Well, cut it.'

His father cut the skin over the whole surface of the abscess. White, liquid pus squirted out and there seemed to be none left.

'You see, daddy, it wasn't so bad as you thought.'

His father kissed and petted him and then went outside to calm down and have another look round.

'You must sleep now,' I said to the boy. 'You know that sleep helps when one is ill.'

He closed his eyes obediently but could not go to

sleep, he was too overwrought. Suddenly something rustled overhead and a cone fell upon us.

'Mother, look, it's a squirrel!' the boy whispered, delighted. Quickly and confidently the squirrel came down and settling on a branch took a peep at us.

'It's your little house, isn't it?' the boy said, forgetting all his troubles. 'You are mistress here, aren't you? Never mind, dear squirrel, we shall soon be gone.'

The squirrel moved its tail and came still closer, watching us attentively with its bright black eyes.

'Mother, it's a good thing that the squirrel has come to us, isn't it?'

'Yes.'

'Why?'

'Because it shows that it hasn't been frightened and that there are no men near.'

'And no dogs?'

'No. Sleep, you are the squirrel's guest.'

'We'll call this place "The Squirrel's House", shall we?'

The boy cheered up completely and went to sleep. The squirrel jumped to the next tree.

Everything around us was as peaceful as it only can be in nature when there is no man about. The grass, the trees, the squirrel, the sun – all lived a pure and serene life of their own. And we – we could at any moment be hounded down by human beings like ourselves but with green stripes and four letters 'OGPU' on their uniforms.

Twentieth century, Socialism, and so much hatred! And after all, what were we guilty of? Of running away from penal servitude to which my husband, innocent, was condemned? In the days of Tsardom convicts were not shot for trying to escape — and what a lot of them did run away! But now, when penal servitude is a hundred times worse than it used to be, we should be killed. And they would first torture us to their hearts' content — and perhaps make the boy look on. No, if we were caught I would resist to the last and be killed straight off.

.

·

CHAPTER VIII

INTO THE UNKNOWN

IN two hours' time the boy woke up. His wound looked healthy, though of course no doctor would have allowed him to walk. But we had to go on. The frontier was near and the guards who had no doubt received a wireless message, must have been hunting for us high and low.

We bandaged the boy's foot and set out towards the mountain pass. He limped, though he walked fairly cheerfully; but we felt sick with anxiety as we looked at him.

The pass seemed near at first, but as always in the mountains, it kept receding into the distance. The trees were getting smaller and further apart and at last disappeared altogether. The slope was quite bare and we could be easily seen from any point at the top.

Our position was so desperate that, had I had my way, I would have flung all precaution to the winds and walked straight on. But my husband insisted that we should run as fast as we could from one block of granite to another, lie there till we got our breath and run to the next shelter.

'Bear up!' we said to the boy. 'We'll rest on the other side of the pass if there are any trees or bushes there, but here you must run as fast as you can.'

I do not know what the boy thought. With a set look

258

on his face he ran, lay down, ran again, and showed neither fear nor hesitation.

We reached the top at last. On the other side the ground sloped gradually; juniper bushes, small firs and birches grew fairly near the top. In the first sheltered spot we could find we threw down our knapsacks and lay down on the soft and almost dry moss.

The country that lay before us was completely unknown to us; we had to consider which way we were to go. A river was flowing to the west. On all the maps which we had seen the frontier ran along the watershed from which a river flowed west. Only one river was marked on the maps, but here we saw two more rivers that were its tributaries. Besides, according to the most optimistic maps, it was at least twenty miles from the end of the valley, which we had left the night before, to the frontier – and here we were looking at the river that flowed west.

'If I only knew where the frontier is, I would run to it at once!' my husband exclaimed.

'They can't catch us at the other side, can they?' the boy asked.

'Yes, they can,' his father answered sternly. 'The OGPU wouldn't scruple to hunt us down in Finland if there were many of them. Last year some prisoners ran away from the works on the Louhi-Kestensky Road and managed to get as far as a Finnish village, but the OGPU guards overtook them and shot them down in the village.

'And what did the Finns do?'

'I don't know. I have heard that when the OGPU guards came home they were shot and declared to be bandits, so that Finland should not make a fuss.

But perhaps they were simply transferred to another post.'

'And shall we soon be in real Finland?'

'Yes. Perhaps in another two or three days. When we feel sure that we have crossed the frontier we shall have a good sleep and walk on quietly. We'll make tea and mushrooms.'

'It will be nice there, daddy, won't it? No one will touch us? Shall we make tea for mother every day?'

'Whenever we want to. But now fetch some water from that pool and let us have a drink before we go.'

We drank some water, slung on our knapsacks and went on.

At first walking was quite easy. Though the trees were small there were so many of them that we could not be seen from anywhere. The ground was almost dry. It sloped evenly towards the bottom of the valley where evidently all the three rivers met. The place was so wild that very likely no one had been here since the creation of the world.

I very much wanted to stop for the night while we were still on dry ground, but we were anxious to cross the valley and reach the next ridge which might possibly mark the frontier. Soon we found ourselves in a real marsh which stretched on either side of the river. Our feet were wet through and we were covered with mosquitoes.

Nothing can be more awful than those Arctic swamps; granite subsoil does not absorb moisture and they stretch for miles and miles. Where there is more soil moss grows on them, sedge and polar birch with thin, wiry branches that conceal deep holes of black water. Small fir-trees grow in batches in drier places where their roots have soaked up some of the moisture. We could only walk holding on to these firs; in the intervals between them we plunged desperately into the squelching moss, almost knee-deep in cold water.

When it grew quite dark we stopped to rest on a damp hillock, utterly exhausted. My husband suddenly said:

'But, anyway, this is much better than standing in a cold corridor outside the examining officer's door.'

'Did you have to stand long?'

'On that particular occasion they called me out of the cell in the evening and said I was not to put on my overcoat. And the examining officer told me to wait outside his door. The sentry would not allow me to walk about. I got so cold that my teeth were chattering and I was shaking as in a fever. The officer went out of his room, then came back again, and I was still standing there. I was aching all over and felt ready to drop, but I knew that other men were made to stand like that for two or three days. So I went on standing. At daybreak I was called at last to the man's rooms. I was trembling all over.

' "What's the matter with you? You seem very upset," he inquired amiably.

' "It's not very warm in the corridor, is it?" I asked angrily.

' "But why didn't you put on your overcoat? I never know how long I may be kept."

' "I was told not to."

' "What idiots! Go back to the cell. I shan't have time to talk to you to-day." '

'When did he let you go, daddy?'

'About six in the morning. I stood there all night.'

'And what happened afterwards?'

'I felt very bad till I got some tea, and afterwards I was sent to the prison kitchen to peel potatoes.'

We forgot that it was cold and that we were standing on a hillock, the three of us.

'I'll try and see if I can find a drier place. You stay here,' said my husband and disappeared in the mist. I very much doubted that he would succeed, but he soon came back:

'This way, please; I've found an hotel, the rooms are ready.'

The joke cheered us up and we readily followed him through the water-logged moss. We were wet up to the knee as it was, and a little more did not matter.

Suddenly we felt something firm underfoot: three huge fir-trees, growing close together, had drained a small bit of ground. We could not see in the mist what was beyond.

·

CHAPTER IX

A TERRIBLE NIGHT

How jolly it was! We chattered light-heartedly, confident that no OGPU could come near us. I rung out all our leg-wrappers, spread them up to dry and re-bandaged the boy's foot in the dark. His wound was not very painful. I covered him up with two coats to keep his feet warm. A cold mist was creeping nearer and nearer. As I had had a sleep on the way I gave my coat to my husband and wrapped up his neck and arms with all the dry rags that I could find. In my cotton dress and overall I curled up under the mackintosh, but before I had had time to doze off I heard my husband groan.

'What is it, dear?'

'I am frozen and I have a dreadful pain.'

He sat there doubled up, shaking all over.

'Where does it hurt?'

'Everywhere. I have pains in my back, in my stomach, I don't know what to do with myself. If only I could get warm!'

It seemed so simple to make a fire, but it was impossible. To light a fire at night when we were close to the frontier! It was out of the question.

His tossing about had made all his wrappings come undone, and his arms and neck were covered with mosquitoes.

What was I to do? On the way he had been bathed in perspiration and kept drinking water out of the marsh. The moment we stopped to rest he shivered with the cold. What was it? Typhoid? Peritonitis? And we were in the wilds, dozens or perhaps hundreds of miles from any Finnish village. We had no wine or spirits of any sort. If only I could give him some hot tea!

In despair I twisted all the rags round him again so as at least to protect him against mosquitoes.

'You must lie down next to me and cover yourself up with the mackintosh.'

'I can't lie down; I am doubled up with pain.'

'Nonsense, you must try. Perhaps you'll be warmer.'

Gradually I induced him to lie on his side so that I could press myself close to him and keep the mackintosh over him, trying to warm the air under it with my breath. The mackintosh reached only to our knees and the mosquitoes were devouring my legs, for while I was attending to him all my wrappings had come undone. But I could not spare a thought for that. No sooner I fancied that the ground and the air inside the mackintosh were beginning to get warm, and his hands felt less stiff and cold, than he would jerk suddenly with an intolerable spasm of pain, and all my microscopic efforts would be wasted. I had to begin all over again, trying to give him all I could of my warmth. It must have been a sheer effort of will that kept me warm, for a cotton dress was certainly not a sufficient portection from the cold.   When he dozed off for a few minutes I hastily began to think.

'What shall we do if in the morning he is too ill to continue the journey?'

Light a fire and make him some tea, and perhaps fix up a warm pack. I could use the oilcloth bag in which we keep the sugar. Rest the whole day and see how he feels.

'If it is typhus or peritonitis, he will himself understand that it's hopeless. We would stay with him to the last. I would make him see what happiness it is to die in the open, a free man and not a convict. After all, we have had four days of freedom, and that has meant so much joy, that if Fate had offered us to buy it at the cost of our lives we should have accepted the bargain without hesitation. Death here is only terrifying because the boy would be left alone.

How can I save him?

If my husband dies I must go back with the boy, because I could not find the way to Finland. We could do the journey back in three days, perhaps less. When we got as far as the timber-works, where we last heard the sound of the axe, I would say good-bye to the boy and send him to the workmen alone. I must tell him to wait till I have gone some distance so that they could not track me, and then throw myself in the river. They might take pity on the boy and not kill him. Yes, that would be the only way to save him. . . .

While I was thinking all this, my husband seemed a little better. He was no longer racked with pain and lay quietly, evidently asleep, though sometimes he groaned slightly. His hands felt warmer. His breath came evenly. I was afraid to stir, though my whole body felt stiff and numb. I was very drowsy, but I dared not go to sleep, as though my conscious will could somehow save my son from blood poisoning and my husband from his mysterious and terrible pain.

CHAPTER X

NO SUN

'Is it light? Time to go?' my husband asked in alarm. 'It's quite early yet. About three in the morning.'

'We must go.' He jumped up and stepped out from under the tree to have a look at the sky.

I snuggled in the warm place under the mackintosh. My night fears and thoughts had gone and I felt calm and happy. I wanted to have if only a few minutes sleep – to sink into unconsciousness as into warm water.

'We must go, it's quite light.'

'It's early. And in this mist you can't see a thing.'

'The sun will soon come out. We did not walk far yesterday.'

'Not far! We walked from three in the morning till nearly midnight.'

'But we rested a lot during the day. I'll go and have a look round while you get ready.'

He was merciless.

I was dreadfully disinclined to move. . . . And it was so difficult to wake the boy! Our leg-wrappings were still damp, the boots were quite wet and it was difficult to pull them on.

My husband came back, pale and anxious.

'Hurry up! The hill we have to climb is not well wooded, we must get there before the sun is up. It's not far to the river.'

266

I was thinking to myself, 'The OGPU or frontier guards are not likely to get up at this hour! They are fast asleep in their warm beds. If only we could have some tea! He does not seem to remember what happened to him in the night. I wonder if it's all nerves?'

It was surprising that the boy was in such good form. He had not had any food for the last twelve hours. I put some rusks in his pocket and gave him a lump of sugar. The wound on his heel had grown bigger after a day's journey, but it did not fester.

We set off, and immediately found ourselves in the marsh once more. Dazzling white moss was all round. and suddenly in this wild spot, within a few yards of our camping-ground which, we thought, was as far off from everywhere as the bottom of the sea, we came across some paths! Two or three paths running from north to south – along the frontier? There were no footprints of any kind, but the paths were clearly marked. We dashed across them, afraid of stepping on a twig or catching at a branch. We walked on breathlessly, without looking back or thinking of anything, intent on getting away as far as we could.

'Now the river will stop us and we shall be done for!' my husband remarked gloomily.

But no, the river was broken up into so many rivulets that we had only to step or jump over them. We sometimes used by way of a bridge rotten tree stumps that had fallen into the river, or simply waded through the water which was not more than knee-deep. Branches of the low-growing Arctic willows got under our feet and caught us in the face as we walked.

We crossed the river. The ascent to the ridge on the opposite bank proved to be as marshy as the valley.

Even in comparatively steep places the thick willow bushes grew among moss hillocks with black water in between. We had to walk on those hillocks though they trembled like jelly as soon as one stepped on them.

There were low white clouds overhead. The sun was trying to come through; one part of the sky began to look lighter than the rest. We stopped and eagerly waited for the sun to come out.

It showed itself, a flat red disk without any rays, and in a minute or two disappeared again without a trace. We could see for the moment where the west was, but it was doubtful if we could keep on walking in the right direction because the wide valley stretched into the distance, winding all the way.

At first we walked fairly cheerfully, hoping that the sun would come out again. We were fearfully thirsty. We had been tramping for five hours without food or drink or rest through swampy ground, rising steeply uphill. We did not feel like eating sugar or bacon. It would have been nice to have some mushrooms* but so far the boy comforted himself by merely pointing to their pretty red caps that were showing everywhere in the white moss. When he found one growing in his path he stroked it and whispered something to it affectionately. In this alien wild expanse mushrooms that he had gathered as a small child seemed like old friends to him.

The sun did not come out. The sky was a uniform white. It was impossible to trace the course of the river that lost itself in the swamps; the ridge that we had seen from the distance disappeared behind the nearer hills; we could not tell whether the slope that

* Edible fungi are meant.   Translator's note.

we were climbing had imperceptibly led us in the wrong direction.

I was feeling so wretched that I was afraid to go near the others. It was I who had ruined them by losing the compass. I was suffering agonies of remorse.

Where were we to go now, when there was no sun to guide us?

My husband was hesitating: he led us sometimes uphill as though hoping to see something in the distance, sometimes came lower, wondering if he could hear the sound of the river which apparently turned to the south.

At last he took one more look at the sky. The clouds had come still lower and crept over the tops of the fir-trees, scattering tiniest drops of moisture over us.

'We cannot go on,' he said. 'It's comparatively dry here. Wait for me, I'll go and find a place to camp in.'

He soon found a good fir-tree. It was in a lovely spot: fluffy white moss covered the ground, tiny bushes of whortleberry with big bluish berries looked like an embroidery on it; the red-capped mushrooms were big as in fairy books; the magnificent fir-trees had a silvery sheen on their soft green needles. Our fir-tree was so exactly like the others and had such thick spreading branches that we could not be seen under it at a distance of ten paces. The ground underneath, soft with the fallen needles, was dry and smooth, and the place looked remarkably cosy.

The child cheered up at once and chattered away:

'Daddy, it's a good thing we stopped, isn't it? We've come a good way to-day. And the rest will do my foot good, won't it? Perhaps it will get quite well. Don't you think it might?'

'Yes, dear, certainly. But I wonder if I shall find any water here. And if we go lower down we shall be in a swamp again.'

'No, don't let us go into a swamp. We can manage without water. I am not a bit thirsty, I was eating whortleberries, they are quite wet and the drops on them taste awfully good. I'll pick some for you, mother. You go to sleep, and I'll go and get some presently.'

I lay down, covering my head with the faithful mackintosh, and the father and the son began a long, friendly conversation, sitting very close to each other.

His father was telling him about his own happy childhood, about journeys by train and by steamer, and the good things one could get to eat at the stations. Then he told him of his expeditions in the mountains, of how he had learned to find his way by the sun and the trees.

'Daddy, but the sun hasn't come out yet,' I heard the boy's voice.

'No, dear, it won't to-day. It will soon be evening, anyhow.'

'And if there is no sun to-morrow either, what shall we do?'

'We'll stay here, under the fir-tree.'

·

CHAPTER XI

FINLAND?

THE day rose but there was not a trace of the sun, The father and the son went to have a look round and brought nearly half a saucepanful of large, moist whortleberries. We sprinkled them with sugar and ate them. Now my husband lay down and I walked about watching for the sun. The sky was white all over. I kept glancing up every two or three minutes but there was no change. Suddenly I noticed a slight movement in the clouds. They lifted and began to part.

'Shall I wake daddy?' the boy asked eagerly.

'Wait a minute.'

A tiny rim of a flat red disk showed between the clouds.

'Run and wake daddy.'

We took our bearings: the valley which led us south the day before, now turned to the west. Further on it turned again, but anyway we could not be certain of our direction for several hours at a time.

Overjoyed, we hastily made ready and walked down towards the river. The bank was overgrown with luxuriant vegetation; a mass of brightly-coloured beetles and butterflies came out in the sunshine. We drank some cold water, which tasted good after twenty-four hours without a drink, and climbed up once more so as not to follow the course of the river which made a large loop.

There had once been a forest fire here: the ground was covered with charred trunks and between them a few tall pine trees stood out.

Nature in these parts lives its own life, going through catastrophes, healing its wounds and hastening to grow masses of flowers and berries while the sun is in the sky for twenty-four hours on end. But it is no place for man; the virgin forest seems to resent intruders.

A whole covey of woodcocks flew suddenly from under our feet.

'I wish I had a gun, we should have had a fine supper!' my husband said with a sigh.

It was very nice walking along the slope, but the river turned sharply to the north.

'We'll have to cross the river. I wish I had thought of it earlier. It may be too deep here,' my husband said.

'But I can swim across, daddy. Only how will mother manage? She doesn't swim very well.'

'I too can swim if it's not too far. Don't you be so superior.'

We came down to the bank. Again the ground grew marshy, willow bushes were in the way, mosquitoes buzzed.

'The water is sure to be icy, I am afraid you'll both catch cold.'

'Nonsense, and, anway, we shall have a good wash. We haven't had a bath for six days.'

The boy did not share my feelings in this respect. He rather enjoyed not having to wash or brush his teeth.

My husband went into the water first. The water was

up to his waist from the first and soon he had to raise above his head the knapsack which he carried in his arms. The water was foaming all round him. We watched his every step.

'The water will be up to my neck,' said the boy.

'It will be up to my shoulders, but the current is so strong I shan't be able to carry anything.'

'Now it's shallower; he is nearly over.'

'He is coming back; make haste and undress. Put your clothes into a bundle, the boots, too, and mind you don't lose your socks.'

'Mother, mosquitoes!'

'Never mind, they won't touch you in the water.'

His father took him across, defending him with his body against the strong current, then came back for me, and crossed the river twice again carrying over our things. The water was icy, and he was shaking with the cold.

'Make haste and dress, we mustn't be long here, it's too exposed,' he said.

'Mother, you are not hurrying!'

'Yes, I am.'

'You are washing your face!'

'You'd better do the same!'

'No, I won't. I'll wash it when we come to Finland.'

'Well, that's silly: you've washed all over and your face is quite grimy.'

Very reluctantly he lifted his mosquito-net and dabbed water on his nose and mouth, blue with the whortleberries.

We were fearfully hungry after our bathe. We had not had a proper meal for six days; now and again we drank water with sugar and ate small pieces of rusks and bacon when we felt faint. We had been too tired to have a real appetite, but now we felt ravenous.

The boy grew quite downhearted.

'It's no joke walking on an empty stomach!'

'We shall soon sit down and have a bite of something. And in the evening we might have some tea.'

'All you care for is tea, but I want a piece of bread.'

'Step along, my dear. There's nothing for it.'

'I am stepping along,' he answered with vexation and went on grumbling to himself. It sounded just like a bumble-bee.

At last we came to a sheltered spot and sat down to have something to eat.

Suddenly I felt that someone was looking at me: a few steps from us stood a huge elk, watching us with a gracious and lordly expression. It was a splendid creature, with beautiful glossy fur. It looked well-groomed, content and dignified. Magnificent spreading horns adorned its head like some wonderful crown. Its dark round eyes were intelligent and attentive.

To attract the attention of the others without alarming the animal, I blew on their necks. They looked up and saw the elk. For a few moments we gazed at him with admiration while he looked at us with serene gravity. Then he walked away, glanced at us once more and disappeared.

'Mother!' said the boy enthusiastically. 'What a beauty! I've never seen one like it.'

'Elks are rare now,' his father said. 'They've been almost exterminated. In Finland it is forbidden by law to hunt elks, but in Russia they do kill them, of course. Last year they killed five hundred and probably more.'

'Do you think it's a Finnish elk, daddy? He looks

proud like an English lord and so well-fed. I am sure he is not from U.S.S.R.'

'It's not easy to tell by the look of an elk what country it belongs to,' my husband said laughing.

It was absurd, of course, but psychologically there was some truth in what the boy said.

In U.S.S.R. everything has been spoiled: the streets are dirty, the houses in need of repair; the rooms damp and grimy; the men are worn out, the dogs are unkempt, the cats are mangy, the pigeons that have not yet been eaten have damaged wings or broken feet. Dirt, hunger, misery are everywhere. There seems to be no beauty or serenity left in U.S.S.R.

'Do you think we can really be in Finland by now?' my husband asked.

'I think so,' I answered. 'The river does flow west on the whole; our maps were on a small scale and probably did not show every bend of it.'

'I can hardly believe it. Well, come along.'

We went on. The slope was steep and dry, covered with a pine forest. There was no undergrowth, not even any whortleberry bushes. The sun was shining brightly and we had no difficulty about our direction.

We must have walked a good twenty miles that day and only stopped when the sun went behind a cloud and a wide, marshy valley lay before us.

'I declare that we are in Finland!' said I. I am not sure that I quite believed it myself, but we badly needed a respite from our anxiety.

For the first time since we escaped we lit a bonfire, though we did it in a deep crevice between the hills. My husband brought huge dry branches and small dead trees, the boy picked up small wood, while I gathered some mushrooms and cooked our first soup.

'Mother, and what are you putting in with the mushrooms?'

'Rice and bacon.'

'But how shall we eat it without bread?'

'It will be very good, you'll see.'

He lay by the fire, dozing, and patiently waited for his supper.

'But how shall we sleep without a fir-tree? It's like sleeping in the street.'

'Never mind, you will sleep by the fire. When it gets cold we'll put more wood on.'

'Will there be enough for the night?' he asked anxiously, used to there never being enough of anything in U.S.S.R.

'Why, look at the lot daddy is bringing.'

He certainly did bring a tremendous heap. We had no axe with us, it would have been too heavy to carry and he had to break off the wood with his hands, like the primitive men.

The warmth of the fire, the bright circle of the flames, the smell of hot food – how wonderful it all was! We felt once more like human beings and not like hunted animals.

'The mushrooms are ready.'

'All right, I'll just make up the fire properly.'

At the top of the small fire over which I had been cooking my husband put a huge tree stump with sticking-out roots, placed some small wood underneath and the flames went up like a big firework.

'What is it?' the boy asked, waking up.

'Our bonfire. Look, isn't it fine? Come and eat your

supper.' We sat down round the saucepan, close together.

'Don't be in a hurry, eat slowly, it's hot,' I warned the boy. With a special feeling of respect for real, hot, satisfying food, we slowly took up in our spoons the thick rice soup with mushrooms and bacon, and ate in small mouthfuls, chewing carefully.

'It's awfully good, mother! Simply delicious!' said the boy in the intervals between two spoonfuls. 'Shall we have supper like that every day now?'

'Yes, certainly. As we walk in the daytime we'll pick mushrooms and then cook them in the evening.'

'And shall we have tea to-night?'

'I think not, dear; it's too far to go to fetch water.'

'Oh, I don't mind, I just mentioned it. I don't want any tea.'

'You darling child,' I thought to myself. 'We've taken you away from home, turned you into a tramp and you look at us with affectionate eyes and are ready to forego all your wishes.'

He dropped asleep the moment he swallowed his last spoonful; his face looked rosy and, as it were, rounder, after food. We sat by the fire, talking.

It was our first real conversation since we escaped. My husband was always talking to the boy, telling him about travels and hunting expeditions, so as to take his mind off the danger we were in. They were constantly noticing ant-heaps, mouse and weasel holes, looking out for squirrels, and the boy, who had never before been in the forest and mountains, was not in the least nervous. My husband knew all the trees, the voices of the birds, the habits of wild animals and their footprints.

But he and I were too uneasy to talk to each other. We both knew only too well what our undertaking meant and what the end of it might be.

Only that evening, by the fire, we ventured at last to speak of what lay before us. A warm and happy sense of intimacy descended upon us; long forgotten thoughts and feelings rose in our minds and our far-off youth seemed to have returned to us once more. Timidly and as it were, shyly, we began to think of the future.

A Soviet intellectual has no future, for the future almost always means prison. There is very little chance of escaping it, since it is not crime that brings one but there 'social origin' and 'social position'. No one in U.S.S.R. wants to think of the next day, let alone making more distant plans; people do not like to talk of the future, knowing that it depends not upon themselves but upon the OGPU.

'Surely they won't send us back from there?' my husband said, almost confidently.

'Of course not.'

To the minds of U.S.S.R. citizens the words 'humanity' and 'humane' hold good outside the confines of their native 'socialistic' state. Everyone knows that it is no use expecting mercy at home; but out there, where free people live, there must be justice and sympathy, and all that does not exist in U.S.S.R.

'Shall we be able to make a living there?' he asked sadly and yet hopefully.

'We shall. If only we come out of this alive, people will help us.'

'We don't know a soul there. Who will help us?'

'Kind people. They won't let us perish, and with a child, too.'

'Ah, I wish I were young! I am not sure that I've got any brains or energy left in me.'

'If you had enough energy to run away from a penal camp, you'll have enough to make your living out there.'

'Yes, I know. I was only wondering. I am certain, at bottom, that I can still do some good work. We'll give the boy a decent education. See how sweetly he sleeps.'

When the boy was asleep his little face assumed an expression of perfect serenity and to us, his parents, seemed the most beautiful thing in the world. But even if somebody from outside could see this bonfire in the wild forest and the child, soft and warm as a kitten, sleeping on the ground as peacefully as though all the angels of heaven were watching over him, he would understand what we must have gone through to risk not merely our own but the child's life for the sake of gaining freedom.

We said good night and lay down by the bonfire. My husband lay behind the boy so as to protect him against the cold that was creeping up from the valley. The black night was all around us; the bright and warm circle by the fire was all that we had so far wrenched from Fate.

.

CHAPTER XII

LOST

THE next day our journey grew more difficult. The beautiful pine forest came to an end and we had once more to go up and down ravines and valleys. The sun came out occasionally, but it was difficult to find the way because the whole place was cut up by mountain ridges, big and small, going in different directions. It was becoming more and more doubtful whether we should ever find the Finnish river which was to guide us.

'The only thing we can do is to go towards the west,' I insisted.

'But we can't go climbing all these mountain chains,' my husband said. 'We must find a good-sized valley and take our bearing from there.'

He and the boy climbed up a hill and came down, very pleased.

'Some ten miles away there's a river which seems to run south, and there's a lot of leafy trees near it. It's a fine valley. If we are in Finland already, we need not be afraid of going south.'

We reached the river after making several *détours* because of marshes, a wide side-stream and so on. We found that it flowed north and if we followed it we would come right back into Russia.

It was a great blow to us. The river bank was one

continuous marsh overgrown with wiry arctic birch. The bank opposite tempted us by its white moss and pretty fir-trees. We decided to wade across to it. We were exhausted, chilled to the bone, got a lot of our things wet, and found ourselves in a worse marsh than ever. We managed to light a bonfire under an up-rooted fir-tree and kept it up through half the night to dry a place where we could sleep.

The morning was damp and foggy.

'We must stay here till the sun comes out,' my husband said.

'We must go on, for we shall never see the sun in this swamp,' I objected.

After much hesitation we decided to go on. We came upon the same river which took another turn, waded across it and climbed uphill.

'I am not going to move from here till the sun comes out,' said my husband.

We lit a bonfire and sadly lay down beside it. It came on to rain several times during the night. Our Soviet waterproofs let water through quite freely. The fire hissed, fighting the rain. It was a bad look-out.

I was awakened by a sharp exclamation of my husband's. He was standing and pointing with a bitter laugh to the flat red disk of the sun rising from behind the very hill which we thought was in the west.

So the whole journey of the previous day had been wasted. We had to wade through the chilly river once more and climb to the place which we had left two evenings before.

A high ridge rising high above the line of the forest, and a perfect chaos of valleys and smaller ridges lay before us. We thought that we had completely lost the Finnish river we were in search of and had no idea how we would find our way. But the boy, whose ideas on geography were distinctly vague, asked cheerfully how soon could we walk to the Bay of Bothnia, for we could not possibly miss that as we missed the river.

We reached the top of the ridge absolutely exhausted. A piercing, icy wind was blowing. The view that lay before us filled us with horror. We had been longing for a green, sunny valley, but instead we saw a huge, gloomy, cauldron-shaped hollow, from which there seemed to be no way out. The forest was all at the bottom, and the slopes were a sheer wall of stone. Far off, on the northern slope, something white looked like a big patch of snow. The heavy clouds crept low, covering the bottom of the hollow like a thick blanket. If we could have turned off anywhere else we would have done so out of the mere fear and repulsion that the place inspired in us but the hollow lay in a western direction and there was nowhere else for us to go.

'We must go down, we shall be frozen here,' I said.

'Once we go down we shall lose our bearings, we must take good stock of the place first,' said my husband.

While we were looking round the boy huddled up behind a stone for shelter, quite subdued.

We did not suspect that we were actually standing on the frontier pass, right over the starting-place of the Finnish river, which we had given up for lost.

But in any case our position was very serious. It had taken us eight days, instead of three or four, to reach the frontier; three-quarters of our provisions, intended for ten days, were gone, and we were beginning to feel exhausted. Though we were safe now from pursuit and from frontier guards, we might easily perish in Finland if we did not find a way out of these wilds and come across human habitation.

.

.

CHAPTER XIII

ONE MAN PER KILOMETRE

Now we dragged ourselves along rather than walked. Our feet were in an awful condition – bruised, swollen, with festering wounds. Before starting a day's march we had to spend no end of time bandaging them; I had to tear up my chemise to make bandages, and every evening we discovered fresh sores.

My husband was the worst off because his boots were falling to pieces. The thin layer of leather on the sole had worn through and showed pieces of birch bark inside. Soviet industry is certainly resourceful!

We were suffering from hunger, too. We reduced our daily portion to two or three tablespoonfuls of rice and two ounces of bacon which we added to the mushroom soup in the morning and evening. The rusks were finished. We had two lumps of sugar a day, one in the morning and one in the evening and the boy had a third in the middle of the day. When we found whortle-berries – and there were very few – we ate some on the spot and picked some to make a hot drink. The worst of all was that salt was coming to an end. If we had plenty of it, we would have cooked mushrooms without adding anything else to them.

A fresh misfortune was the cold. A north wind was blowing continually, and we were simply frozen in the night if we could not find enough dry wood to feed the fire all the time.

On one of those cold nights my husband had another attack of pains and in the morning he found he could not use his left arm. He felt breathless and when the pains came on again was not able to walk. We thought it was probably his heart. Overstrained by the life in the penal camp, by our march (we were already twelve days on the way) and the heavy weight he carried, it might give way any day. And what would become of us then?

Our only salvation would be to meet someone. We talked of nothing but where and how we could find any people. There were no traces of trees being cut, the forest was quite untouched, though it proved to be in a fine, broad valley and not in a hollow between the mountains, as we had thought at first; the river flowing through it was big, and had many tributaries.

It was our son who brought us the first message of hope.

'Daddy, there's a mark of an axe!' he cried in an almost frightened voice.

Indeed, an old tree in the depths of the forest had been marked by an axe, evidently some time ago.

'Very clever of you to notice it! Yes, that's the first sign of man we have seen. So, evidently people do come here sometimes.'

'Certainly, daddy! After all, there must be people in Finland.'

'They all drift towards the south-west; here in the north, the population is one man per square kilometre. Imagine what it means if you have a village with a hundred inhabitants and a hundred square kilometres of land around it.'

Two hours later we came upon a clearing in the forest. It must have been made ten or fifteen years ago because it was covered with young growth; most of the trees had been taken away. Finally, the boy found a neat little peg with a Roman figure on it, probably indicating the number of the plot.

'Yes, dear,' said my husband with a sigh, 'in Russia they now destroy forests wherever they can without any system or order, and here, you see, everything is planned and numbered.'

The following day, as we were skirting round a marsh, the boy saw two poles of equal height at the edge of it.

'Look, daddy, what is this?'

Sore as our feet were, we went to look. There was a third pole, also with a pointed and charred end. It was an arrangement for drying hay. Close by there were evident signs of man's presence: traces of two big bonfires, remains of a shelter made of branches, a wooden box and a torn shirt.

'Daddy, just look, they've thrown away a box that's been nailed together! They hadn't even troubled to take the nails out! They must be a bourgeois lot!'

'I expect they have nails enough in this country,' said his father, laughing. 'But surely if they come here for hay, the village can't be more than twenty or thirty miles off. I wonder why there is no sign of haymaking – the grass is fine, and this is the twentieth of August.'

We had no idea that in this part haymaking does not begin till September, when harvest has been gathered in. The ground is so moist that the grass remains fresh all the summer.

A day later we made a discovery which seemed to us of enormous importance: we found a fence. A real, well-built, high fence, going from north to south across a beautiful forest.

How absurd it was to climb a fence in these wilds! The boy was very much amused at the clumsy way in which I did it while he climbed over it several times for the mere pleasure of doing it.

We were certain that we should soon find a path. Surely people did not build fences at an indefinite distance from their homes!

We traced that fence for at least a mile each way and discovered nothing.

We learned afterwards that villagers living a good hundred miles away built that fence so that their deer, which they let off to pasture in the forest in the summer, should not cross over to the Russian side. Late in the autumn when the snow is on the ground, they come to fetch the animals whom they need in winter for drawing their sledges.

The forest was as wild as ever and there was no more trace of man. There were endless paths made by elks, so well trodden that one could walk on them for about an hour as on a garden path. But these paths either went down to the river or led to open spaces where elks play and rest.

'If there are so many elks about, it means there are no men near,' my husband warned us.

We found one day fresh traces of a bear; but there was no sign of man. We had already slept four times in this valley; with the most stringent economy our food

could not last us more than another five or six days,
and we made less and less progress every day. My
husband suffered dreadfully. Time after time his pain
caused him to lie down when the journey was quite
easy, and we had to stop till he was better – and that,
when we could not afford any delays.

'How dreadful to have got ill just now! How can I
bring you out of these wilds?' This thought made him
suffer perhaps more than his pains.

Now that we were in Finland, on a big river, and
bound to come to some dwelling sooner or later, everything depended on whether his heart would last out
till then. We still had a few lumps of sugar and a few
pieces of bacon left. Should we be able to walk when
these were gone?

We were walking on the slope trodden down by elks
when the boy cried suddenly:

'Daddy, a bottle!'

It was only the bottom of a bottle, but it certainly
was an eloquent sign of man. Further along we found a
heap of last year's hay, horse droppings, a blue rag.
Three clear paths went from this place in different
directions. It was a beautiful forest all round –
splendid tall pines.

'Daddy, which path shall we take?' the boy asked
excitedly, as though we were coming to a house for
certain.

'The middle one, it is the most used of the three.'

'A cutting, a fresh one!'

The trees must have been felled only a few days ago,
there was still a smell of freshly cut wood. Some of it
had not yet been taken away. Had we come here two
or three days ago we might have met the woodcutters.

'Daddy, how nice it is here! What a jolly place!' the boy said with animation. 'Look, there's a lake over there, and granite rocks round it, and pines. In our geography book there was a picture "A Forest Lake in Finland", very much like it.'

The path, well trodden, but with no fresh traces of man, apparently led to the river. We could tell its presence by the thick growth of young elm, but we could not hear it; it flowed quietly and peacefully.

'A house!'

It was not a house but a low log hut, open on one side and roofed in with planks, sloping towards the open side. There was a shelf inside on which several dates and Finnish names were written. We did not see any names of places. The dates went fifteen and twenty years back, so there was no doubt that the place was well-known and that people came here. But when and what for?

There were two charred tree-trunks in the open part of the hut, but they must have been lying there since the summer before, for they were overgrown with moss.

People could not be very far off, but how were we to find them when we had so little strength left and so few provisions!

'I'll see if I can catch some fish,' said my husband and went to the river.

The boy lit a fire and put the saucepan on to make tea. We very much wanted to stay here and spend the night under a roof.

'Shall we camp here, mother?' the boy asked pleadingly.

'We shall see how daddy is. If he is well, we must go on, and if not we'll put up here for the night.'

'It's very nice here, isn't it? We shall soon come to a real house now, shan't we?'

'Yes, I expect we shall.'

·

CHAPTER XIV

AT DEATH'S DOOR

My husband did not catch any fish, but he was rested and we went on. That was a terrible mistake. We ought to have thought it all out carefully and looked round, but we frivolously concluded that having found the hut we would soon discover a road. Things went against us almost at once: the path from the hut grew narrower, almost disappeared among the elm bushes, appeared again and kept losing itself in the marsh. We struggled on for the rest of the day and spent the night on a tiny island in the biggest swamp we had ever seen. It extended in the westerly direction like an emerald sea. It took us away from the river and, in trying to skirt round it, we went further and further south. We very much wanted to go back to the hut; it seemed incredible that there was no path from it at all. We must have made a mistake somewhere. We should probably have returned, but we were deceived by traces of horse's hoofs which we found on the path that had reappeared again. They were quite fresh, the horse was shod, and it looked exactly as though someone had just ridden there. But the path led us to a marsh and disappeared completely.

We had no idea that the Finns let their horses pasture in the forest, like the deer, and that the hoof-marks we saw were made by horses wandering at random or following an occasional path.

We might have been more careful if my husband had felt ill and had had to count every extra step, but as soon as he found himself in difficulties he thought of nothing but going on and his pains left him – that's his temperament. The harder the way the faster he walked. At last the slope along which we were going turned sharply to the south-east and it became obviously senseless for us to continue our journey. It was bitter to confess to ourselves that we had lost a whole day and the only thing to do was to find the shortest way back. Walking through endless swamps reduced the boy's feet and mine to such a condition that we could scarcely drag ourselves along. We had to spend the night far away from the hut, which seemed to us now the key to all our future.

My husband found a clearing and kept up a huge blaze all night, burning the logs that had not been taken away. He was hoping that a forester might see the smoke and the flames. Who would have supposed that there were no foresters there at all, and the horses wandered about by themselves!

As soon as it was light, my husband went on ahead to scout. It was useless to protest: when he felt an access of energy, he had to work it off. My chief comfort was that he could walk so well again, forgetting all about his pains; for the last few days I had been in terror that he would not get up at all after one of those attacks.

The boy and I lay sadly by the burnt-out fire. He was cutting faces on the big mushrooms that were too old to be cooked – a Chinaman with slanting eyes, a

square-jawed sailor, a fat bourgeois, a hungry proletarian. Then he fixed them up on sticks and placed
them in a row. Probably, playing is as necessary to
children as thinking is to grown-ups; but he was very
slow and sad at his game. Our tramp the day before
had evidently been too much for him.

His father came back in high spirits – the hut was
within two hours walk.

But what an agony that walk was! One swamp after
another – now full of small hillocks overgrown with
small wiry birches, now one green quivering mass of
slime. Gasping for breath and bathed in perspiration
we walked for over four hours instead of two and when
we reached the hut at last we sank on the ground in
utter exhaustion. We put off all decisions till the following day, at the moment we wanted nothing but rest. It
was clear now that the paths from the hut did not lead
anywhere and were only used for hunting or fetching
the deer; people evidently came here by water.

A paper bag which we found in the corner of the
hut created one more illusion for us: it had written on
it 'The Kulojarvi Stores'. We remembered the name
Kulojarvi and wanted to get there, because on our old
maps there was a cart-track leading south-west from
there. We thought it could not be far off, if a paper bag
from there had been brought into the forest.

As a matter of fact, the cart-track was by now a fine
road used by motors; many new villages had been built
north of Kulojarvi, but the nearest of them lay a good
seventy-five miles from where we were. In a civilized
country bottles and paper are not a treasure as in
U.S.S.R. and may be often found far from a dwelling.
The conclusions we had drawn were quite absurd; it is

not safe even for educated people to be cut off from the world for fifteen years and see nothing but Soviet newspapers.

That night only the boy slept, but how heart-rending it was to look at him! He lay there without moving, his head was thrown back, his arm was bent awkwardly, as though his body did not belong to him. Children sleep like that when they have been weakened by a serious illness. His face was drawn, his little nose looked thin and sharp, blue veins showed on the temples in spite of the sunburn. Only two days before he had looked well, but his strength gave way and all at once he became small, frail and pitiful.

My husband sat most of the time by the bonfire sucking his empty pipe. There was very little tobacco left. I did not want to ask him what he was thinking – I had nothing comforting to say to him.

When in the morning we sat down to our saucepan of mushroom soup he glanced at our feet. We did not put on our boots and stockings till the last moment so as not to chaff the sores that now covered our feet and ankles. My husband said sharply:

'You cannot go on.'

The boy glanced at him in alarm. I, too, did not understand at first what he was driving at.

'Listen,' he went on. 'You must both stay here, in the hut. It's a noticeable place, everyone must know it. I'll go by myself and find a village or a house much quicker. I cannot drag you through these marshes any more. I cannot bear to see you struggling on when you can hardly walk. If I go alone I need not pick my way and will find people in a couple of days; then I will come to fetch you and bring back some food.'

It was so unexpected that I said nothing. Mastering my emotions I was trying to consider the matter objectively.

(1) Alone, he will walk quicker if he does not have an attack of his pains. If he has, he may die on the spot; we shall not know, and remaining here we shall certainly perish also.

(2) If he gets to a village not in two but in five or six days, we shall still be alive by the time he comes back; if we stay quietly in the hut and feed on boiled berries we shall not die of starvation. There will still be some life left in us.

(3) If we continue the journey, the three of us, the question is will the child stand it? His pulse was weak and irregular; he was obviously overstrained.

(4) What should I do in his place? Go on by myself, clearly.

While I was thinking the boy glanced anxiously at his father who gazed into the fire without turning to look at me. He knew it would not be easy for me to remain behind in the forest, doing nothing, and perhaps perish with the boy, because, waiting for him, we should eat our last crumbs of provisions and be too weak to go in search of help.

'Go,' I said, 'I am certain you will save us.'

Deeply touched, he looked at me gratefully and kissed both my hands blackened by the weather, the smoke and the mushroom juice. My gloves had been torn and lost long before. The boy hugged and kissed his father, who now talked cheerfully and made plans.

'I'll go into the first house I come across. . . .'

'You'll frighten them; they'll take you for a bandit,' the boy joked him.

'Really?' my husband asked me anxiously. 'Do I look very alarming?'

'You are rather a sight, but you look more like a tramp than a bandit. I think they'll take pity on you and not be afraid.'

'Well, I'll go in, ask what the village is called, tell them about our hut. . . .'

'But they won't understand you,' the boy said doubtfully.

'I'll draw it all: the river, the felled trees, the hut, you and your mother. Then I'll ask where the shop is where I can buy you some food.'

'How can you? You have no money.'

My husband looked at me questioningly.

'Take my wedding-ring, they may give you something in exchange.'

'Good. Besides, it will be a proof that I am not a tramp. And you,' said he turning to the boy, 'give me your note-book and photograph.'

It was the boy's last photograph, taken just before we set out. A round healthy little face; only a shadow of it was left now – sweet, touching and dreadfully pitiable.

'Now let us put down in your diary on which day I go. What is the date to-day?'

We could not reckon it up at once. The last few days of fatigue and anxiety seemed merged into one. We set out on our journey on August 8th. We would remember that day all our lives. We had been sixteen days on the way. How many more days would the journey take us? How many more days had we to live at all?

'What may I take with me? How much sugar have we left?'

'Ten lumps,' said I, though we really had only seven.

'I'll take one.'

'Nonsense, you must take at least two.'

'But I'll get to a house and have something to eat before you do.'

'Mind you get a good meal, daddy.'

After many protests on his part, I cut for him a piece of bacon that could not have weighed more than two ounces. I was beginning to lose patience.

'Everything depends on your getting there, and you make all this fuss. We'll be all right here.'

'But I can manage for several days without food. I've done it often enough in the camp. I don't want anything except perhaps some salt. Have you any to spare?'

'Yes,' I answered firmly, scraping together two teaspoonfuls, of which I gave him one.

There was nothing more to give him.

He was in a hurry to get off. It was a terrible moment when the father, pale, thin, with a dishevelled beard, discoloured by the sun, and hands covered with burns and bruises, gave a last hug to the boy. The child looked very frail; there were dark hollows round his eyes and his lips were white and drawn.

'Good-bye, daddy! Come back soon, daddy!'

'How many days shall we wait?' I asked the dreadful question.

'Five: three days to get there, and two days back; the journey back will not take so long.'

'I shall wait six. What shall I do then?'

'Make bonfires in the clearing, perhaps someone will see the smoke. . . . I will come back. Good-bye.'

He went away. We stood looking after him till he disappeared among the trees. The place was strange without him – still and empty. The forest seemed bigger and we felt smaller and more helpless.

'What shall we do, mother?' the boy asked sadly.

'Let us lie down and put our feet in the sun, that's the best way to heal the wounds. When daddy comes back we shall have to walk again. And we must put everything in order, we shall be here a long time.'

'Let us make it look like a room!' said the boy wistfully. Poor child, how he longed for something like a home! He was delighted when we put on the shelf his little clock with a luminous face, by which he had learned as a baby to recognise the hour of eight at which he was allowed to get up and make a noise. We also had with us a china cup and three silver spoons. Our provisions – five lumps of sugar, a tiny piece of bacon, two or three ounces of rice and a teaspoon of salt were carefully packed in an oilcloth bag and hidden in the corner to keep them safe from any animals that might stray into the hut in our absence.

Though it was morning the boy soon went to sleep, and I sat beside him, thinking. He had often lain like this, struggling against serious illness, while I sat by him watching for the least gesture or movement to tell me how he was. He had his own way of being ill: the greater the danger he was in, the more sweet and patient he was. Once he reduced to tears the doctor who had to operate on him. It was the same thing now: he lay on the ground with an empty sack under his head, sadly and quietly. He had given up for his father's freedom all that he held dear in his childish life, and now he was at death's door.

The sun was warming his sore feet; on the heel there was the scar from the abscess, not quite healed yet and broken water blisters were festering. No, he certainly could not have walked any further.

I had to go and pick some berries, though I was hardly able to pull on my boots, my feet hurt me so. In the forest I suddenly felt horribly depressed. I seemed to hear my husband's voice, a groan, and some mysterious distant music.

'Mother! Mother!' It was the boy calling me pitifully.

'What is it, dear? I am here.'

'Mother, come here, I feel rather miserable.'

I came back and made a hot drink of whortleberries and red bilberries.

'I wish we had gone with daddy! I am quite rested and could have walked slowly.'

'It was better for him to go alone,' was all I could say. After a hot drink he went to sleep again, with a tired look on his little face.

I had to pick some mushrooms for supper. It was a good thing that the berries and the mushrooms grew quite close to the hut.

How long the hours were! I seemed to be conscious of every minute passing and falling like a heavy drop into the past.

'Mother! Mother! Where have you gone to again?'

'Only to pick some mushrooms, darling. Lie still, I am quite close to you.'

'I feel very miserable.'

'Sing.'

He began to sing. This had been his chief comfort during the last few days: he would sit down, hugging his knees, and sing all his school songs, then the Red

Army songs. Now he sang with special feeling the melodramatic songs that beggar boys sing in suburban trains:

> "Soon soon I'll be dead,
> They will bury me,
> No one will know
> Where my grave shall be.
> No one will know,
> No one will come.
> But in the early spring
> The sweet nightingale
> Will come and sing."

He was probably not thinking of the words, but I could not refrain from tears. My darling boy, shall I really have to bury you here? If you only knew how near the truth your song was!

'Mother, I've sung them all.'

I had to return.

'Would you like to help me to clean the mushrooms?'

'No, I'd rather not. May I lie closer to you?'

'Do.'

It was not very convenient for getting on with my job, but I was glad to feel his head pressed against my side.

'Now you must stir the soup and look after the fire, and I'll go to fetch some more wood, or we'll freeze in the night.'

There were lots of logs and branches lying about. I brought in heaps and heaps of them, badly scratching my hands, but I knew that all this burned very quickly; the chief thing was to find two tree-trunks that would keep the fire going all night. At first I thought I could not move them at all; then I dragged them for two paces and fell down, but eventually they were in the hut though my arms and legs were trembling with the effort. Our supper was ready, but the boy could not swallow more than two or three spoonfuls.

'I can't eat; it makes me rather sick.'

'Here's a little salt for you; put it on your palm and when you begin to feel bad, have a lick.'

'Right. Yes, it tastes quite good.'

We got through our supper in this way and the boy went to sleep. Now I understood what keeping up a fire through the night means! At first the branches caught quickly, throwing off a tremendous heat, and I dropped asleep, overcome by the warmth; then the fire died down, the cold of the night crept nearer and nearer, but I had not the strength to wake up. At last, when I opened my eyes, it was dark, bright stars were shining in the clear sky, the burnt branches showed black, and the two tree-trunks underneath crackled, sending up pungent white smoke. I had to make haste and put some more on; the branches were all tangled into a heap, and if I put on too many I could not blow up the fire. I felt very sorry for myself, but could not give up the job because the boy was shivering in his sleep. I broke up some twigs, shovelled the hot embers under them, put branches at the top and blew, and blew, and blew. The white ashes flew about in flakes, clouds of white smoke rose up, two or three tongues of pale orange flame showed through the smoke and the whole heap blazed up suddenly.

That sort of thing went on all night, almost every half-hour.

How I longed for morning, sunshine and steady warmth! Meanwhile, in the cold light of the moon everything sparkled with silvery hoarfrost.

Our second day began late – the child did not wake till nine having gone to sleep at seven the evening before. I had burnt up all my supplies of firewood, my hands were black and grey, but, anyway, the boy had been warm while he slept.

'I wonder where daddy is now?' he said with a sigh as soon as he woke up. 'I could have walked all right to-day.'

But when I made him wash himself and then put him out in the sun he dropped asleep again.

The second, the third and the fourth days were exactly like the first. The boy kept awake only for a couple of hours in the evening. We sat side by side on one of the overcoats covering ourselves up with the other and talked. He wanted me to tell him about foreign countries, about the towns, the houses, the trams; he longed for people and would not look at the pine trees. As for me, it was only the beauty around us that saved me from black misery. It would have been horrible to wait for five days in a prison cell without knowing whether he would save us. But here the rustle of the forest, the splashing of the river, the wonderful peace of it all, made me conscious of forces so much greater than man, that nothing in me rebelled or protested.

> "All is well; for waking or sleep
> The hour will come as is fit."

But I wanted to live all the same . . . especially when I listened to the boy telling me of his childish joys and exploits.

It was a great feat to be the first to run out of the classroom and to arrive at the communal kitchen

across the road. By no means all children could go to
the communal kitchen and the privilege was highly
prized.

'You see, it was very lucky: Petka had a card of
admission because his father is a workman, though he
makes three hundred roubles a month, and I had one
because though you were a civil servant, you had only
a hundred and twenty roubles a month. If you earned
one hundred and fifty I couldn't have had a card. And
dinner was ever so much better there than at school.'

It would have been impossible to explain to him that
in capitalistic countries sons of civil servants and workmen and even of tradespeople and priests had an equal
right to food. He would not have believed it.

'And, you know, one day I got two meat rissoles
instead of one! We only had meat rissoles once or twice.
But before Christmas we could eat as much bread as we
liked, and afterwards they gave us only one slice and
cut it ever so thin, too! And how I should love to have a
piece of bread now, mother! Just a little crust! I would
eat it in tiny little bites. Is it really true you can buy as
much bread as you like abroad?'

'Yes, provided you earn the money to buy it with.'

'And is it cheap?'

'Yes.'

'Shall I be able to send a little to Petka?'

'Yes.'

'What day of the month is it?' he asked suddenly.

'Twenty-seventh.'

'School will begin soon. All the boys will be back and
I won't be there. They'll think I am ill. What will
Mishka say? He may have heard that I ran away
because his father is in the OGPU.'

When we exhausted our subjects of conversation we began to sing in an undertone all that we remembered. He grew drowsy as darkness came on and putting on his cap and two pairs of socks – all his night-toilet consisted in – settled down to sleep, and said:

'Now sing "O give me, give me back my freedom" from *Prince Igor* . . . that's about daddy. And the "Evening" from the *Queen of Spades*, and the "Sleep Song" from *Sadko*. You remember how you used to play Chopin's Concerto for me?'

He went to sleep, and I began my nightly job of feeding the fire and thinking my thoughts.

The next day would be the sixth since he left. If he did not return, we should have to set off after midday. What should I say to the boy? How could we go, knowing that his father had perished?

The boy was the first to wake up that morning.

'Will daddy come back to-day, mother?'

'I don't know, dear; perhaps to-morrow.'

'You know, we have one lump of sugar left? Don't let us eat it till daddy comes back.'

'Very well.'

'Only, please, mother, don't go away.'

'But I must pick some berries to make our tea.

'Then I'll stand by the hut and sing, and you answer me.'

'All right.'

I wandered about and he stood by the hut and sang. His clear voice echoed down the river, and sometimes I called back to him.

He called to me once:

Mother, listen, there are voices!'

'No, darling, it's your fancy.'

During those days we had heard voices, and singing, and music, but it was all an hallucination.

'Please, don't go away, mother,' he said anxiously.

'I'll come to you in a minute, I'll only pick the bilberries under that pine tree.'

I went a little way, to hear the better. Voices. Loud men's voices. It was not he. If it had been he, he would have let us know by calling in his own special way.

CHAPTER XV

THE PRICE OF DELIVERANCE

'Mother!' the child cried with all his might.
I was already running to the hut.

Two men in military uniform were coming out of the forest at a quick pace. But where was *he*? There! He was staggering, his face looked dreadful, black and swollen and there was some dry blood near the nose.

'Darling, darling!' We held his hands again, the boy was kissing and stroking him.

He sank helplessly on the logs without looking at us.

'Dearest, what has happened?'

'I had a fall and hurt myself. Give me some water.'

'Here, daddy, have a drink. Mother will make tea directly; we saved up one teaspoonful and a lump of sugar.'

'They have a little with them,' he said, speaking with difficulty, pointing to one of the Finnish frontier guards, who were looking at us somewhat disconcerted. 'They wouldn't let me buy any food — they said they'd take plenty, but they have eaten most of it themselves.'

'What does it matter! The chief thing is that we are saved. All will be well.'

'It took me two days to get there, though I had nothing to eat and my boots had fallen to pieces. They thought they would walk quicker than I did, but I could scarcely drag them here! They took three days on the way.'

Naturally, they could not walk like a man who is trying to save all that he holds dear in life.

There was a rattle in his throat, he coughed and fresh blood showed on his handkerchief that was already stained with red.

'I hurt myself when I fell,' he said guiltily.

'Was the journey difficult?'

'Very. A lot of stones.'

The boy hugged and kissed his father and was almost in tears. He could not understand what the matter was – why was daddy so strange, as though he weren't glad.

Meanwhile the Finns cooked some oatmeal porridge. They shared it with us in a brotherly way and also gave each of us a piece of black bread. It is curious that only the taste of real food makes one understand how hungry one is. We felt that we could have sat there eating for a long, long time. But the porridge was soon gone.

'How are your feet? Can you walk?' my husband asked. 'Their provisions are coming to an end; we'll have to hurry.'

'Yes, we can walk all right. Our feet are much better.'

I was sorry my husband could not have a day's rest in the hut before setting out again, but there was nothing for it.

Now the Finns walked in front, carefully preparing the way – chopping off branches and placing tree-trunks across streams. The boy walked behind them, and my husband and I came last. I was afraid that he would fall, he was so weak.

When we were among the thick elm and willow bushes some five hundred yards away from the hut, my husband asked me:

'Did one of you sing?'

'Yes. The boy sang, and I answered him.'

'Just at this spot I heard your voices but I thought it was my fancy. I had imagined so many times that I heard you talking and singing. But this time it was wonderfully clear. These men had been making difficulties since yesterday, they were frightened and decided that I was a Bolshevik, leading them into a trap. This morning they gave me two hours: if we did not reach the hut within that time they would turn back and make me go with them or kill me. Two hours had passed and they began to bar my way. And suddenly I heard a voice, it was the boy singing. Then the wind carried it away. I lost my head completely and started to run towards the sound. I fell, scrambled on to my feet, and ran again. They would certainly have shot me, but then they too heard the voice. I was in such an agony of despair that I am not myself yet. . . . Had they turned back you would have both perished. You could never have found your way alone, and to-day is the sixth day, so you would have concluded that I was dead. And indeed I would have been dead, for I certainly would not have turned back alive. I've never lived through anything more terrible. . . . Now they will lead us to safety; but I can't get over it yet.'

'You will, in time,' said I. 'The only thing that matters is that you have saved us and that if we live it will be thanks to you.'

·

CHAPTER XVI

BACK TO CIVILISATION

IT was incomparably easier to walk when we had two
strong men with a good axe to help us. When we put
up for the night they chopped plenty of enormous logs
and had no difficulty in keeping up the fire. The
following day the way was easier: we often came across
well-trodden paths, burnt out places, cuttings in the
forest. Small hills were red with big ripe bilberries; in
the birch woods we found bushes of raspberry and red
currants. Horses with big bells round their necks ran
out of the forest and looked at us from the other side of
the river.

'That's the creature that deceived me,' said my
husband. 'I lost my knife through them. I sat down
to peel some mushrooms and suddenly heard the
sound of a bell. I rushed to see – there was no one,
and in my excitement I must have left the knife
behind.'

'But what did you eat, daddy?'

'Nothing at all. I had a drink of water now and
again and went on. I tried to bake mushrooms on
the fire, but they tasted so horrid I couldn't swallow
them.'

'And mother cooked a lovely soup one day. You
know, I got quite sick of eating mushrooms, and
mother made a soup with what remained of rice and

bacon, and we also found a handful of crumbs in the rusk bag. It was awfully good.'

Towards midday we came to a big and very beautiful river. The high hills on either side were covered with a splendid forest. It would have been very difficult to walk here because the sloping banks were piled with blocks of granite. The men put us in a boat and rowed us down the river.

It was anything but a quiet journey: every quarter of an hour we came upon rapids and recovered our peace of mind only after emerging from them. First we heard a dull roar and saw big stones showing from the water; the boat was sucked in by the stream, and the water boiled up suddenly, foaming and seething; the boat, thin as a shell, was tossed about, carried against the stones and past them. One of the Finns rowed with all his might without looking right or left, the other leaned out as far as he could to see better, shouted something in a wild voice and guided the boat with his oar. I cannot think how it was that we safely passed each time these awful rapids. All that was required of us was to sit perfectly still at the bottom of the boat until we were in calm waters once more.

In normal circumstances I should have considered such a journey a perfect madness because some of the rapids were like real waterfalls, but since we were being taken in the boat, I thought no more about it. Anyway, it was more comfortable than climbing and hurting one's feet against the granite.

The parts where we had been vainly looking for people were so deserted because the river was the only means of communication, and the rapids made it inaccessible. People only went there for hay, timber and fish. There was a big rich village below the rapids, but in the upper reaches of the river marsh and forest stretched for hundreds of miles.

Our race over the rapids continued till late in the evening.

'This is where I spent my second night,' my husband said, pointing to a place.

'Did you make a fire?' asked the boy, who was growing more and more impressed by his father's exploit.

'Yes, but it soon went out. I couldn't be bothered. I was chilled to the bone and as soon as it was light, I went on. And at this spot my boots fell to pieces. Beyond this bend of the river there are some huts and poles for drying hay. When I saw some cow droppings here, I ran on like mad. Do you see that fence and house over there? It turned out to be a barn. The first house you come to is more than two miles from here. They have a funny arrangement here: houses are fenced in all round, without any gate or opening; there are some steps fixed to the fence for people to climb over. It's to prevent cattle getting into the yard. At first I felt very shy about climbing a fence.'

'Were they frightened of you, daddy?'

'No. They are a very kind people. In that house there was only a woman with a child. She took me across the river to a peasant who remembered a little Russian. How clean their houses are! Simply spotless. Curtains over the windows, pots with flowers on the window-sills.'

'Daddy, and did they give you something to eat?'

'Yes, they did. They gave me milk – I believe I drank a whole jugful – and curds and bread. They began making coffee, but just then the frontier guards rode up on their bicycles.'

'What a pity!' the boy said sympathetically.

'Why, you silly, I was in a hurry to get back to you.'

'Still, you should have had some coffee. And what then?'

'They took me to their office. I explained everything to them, drew a map and showed your photograph. They liked it very much. Then the senior guard asked me to take off my knapsack. I thought they wanted to search it. I didn't care, there was nothing but woollen stockings and wet leg-wrappings in it.'

'And what did they do?'

'It seems they packed it with provisions.'

'How splendid! Sensible people! '

'Another funny thing was, I kept telling him that I must go with them for they would never find you without me, and he was saying something in Finnish. At last he lost patience, put my knapsack on my back and pointed to the door, and off we went.'

The boy was highly amused.

'Daddy, and where are they taking us now?'

'To the frontier guards' office.'

'And will they give us something to eat?'

'Sure to.'

We landed when it was quite dark, and walked quickly down a sandy road. It was warm walking, but we were quite frozen sitting still in the boat all day. There was a smell of fresh straw: in the darkness we could barely distinguish huge stacks of barley in the fields.

The village was a good two miles long; all the houses

were in darkness; we were the only people in the
street.

We stopped at last before a clean-looking house
with a high porch. The shutters were closed but sounds
of a gramophone playing a gay waltz came from
within. Our guides knocked at the door; it flew open.
Cries of welcome together with the loud waltz greeted
us, while two huge dogs barked on the steps.

We could not make out how many people there were
and what they were doing.

It was a big room with a huge stove, a stand for
rifles and two tiers of iron bunks, neatly covered with
clean counterpanes, checked white and blue. There
was a large deal table and benches.

One feels awkward in a room after such a journey
as ours. Everything was clean, neat and tidy, and we
were wet and dirty and looked like scarecrows. In
all this noise and commotion, my son and I rightly
guessed who the most important person in the place
was.

Small and thick-set he kept running in and out of
the kitchen. His movements were full of such meaning
that the boy could not take his eyes off him.

'Mother, what is he turning?'

'A coffee-mill; he is grinding coffee-beans.'

The boy could not understand: he had never seen
real coffee – since he was born we had only barley or
baked oats coffee.

'Look what he is bringing!' the boy almost shouted.
'A plate full of butter! Just look! Whatever is he going
to do with it?'

Presently this delightful cook, whom we shall never
forget, invited us to the kitchen to have coffee. A fire

was burning brightly in the oven, saucepans were boiling on the top, and by the window a small table was spread with a white tablecloth, china cups with a design of flowers were set for each one of us, with a sugar basin and a cream jug in the middle. The rolls in the bread basket were so white that the boy felt a little doubtful about them.

And all this in a frontier guards' barracks!

We sat at the table drinking real fragrant coffee, while the cook stirred something in a big saucepan, chatting to us amiably in an incomprehensible language.

'What is it, mother?'

'Macaroni.'

'But it is white?'

Soviet macaroni is grey because it is made with unsieved flour, so he was puzzled by it.

Meanwhile the cook opened two tins of pork and turned them out into the saucepan.

'Well, I never!' said the boy.

After that he did not want to leave the kitchen at all and only ran out of it for a minute to tell me in great excitement:

'Do you know what he did with that butter? Would you believe it; he put it into the macaroni! Well, they certainly are not starving in Finland! You know, they wrote in *Lenin's Sparks* that the peasants here have no bread and run to us, to U.S.S.R. Not likely!'

Soon the cook set the big table for supper, brought black bread, butter, milk and a huge tureen of macaroni. All sat down and began eating quietly and decorously. The boy ate slowly and seriously.

'It's a good idea to have cold milk on the table,' he

remarked. 'It's a great help – one takes a drink, and then can eat a little more.'

When the meal was over the cook went to wash up; somebody brought for my son and me a large hay-bag, a pillow and a woollen blanket. My husband was given a vacant bunk on the top tier. The others got into their bunks and put out the light.

'Mother, how nice, how warm, how soft!' said the boy as he dropped off to sleep.

.

CHAPTER XVII

WHERE'S THE CRISIS?

Now we were thoroughly taken care of: we were fed, driven from place to place, delicately questioned about our past and soon dispatched to Helsingfors. We were not yet allowed to mix freely with the Finnish citizens, so our impressions on the way were only derived from what we saw; but life in U.S.S.R. teaches one to see things which others would leave unnoticed.

In the village beyond the Arctic circle we saw stacks of barley, good cows, well-built, warm houses. A fine road ran through marshes, forests and rocks. Wherever possible, marshes were drained and bits of forest converted into arable land. Red farmhouses with white shutters had flower-gardens in front of them. Those farms evidently belonged to new settlers who must have toiled desperately to clear their land from tree-stumps and stones. The small Finnish nation, waging a stubborn fight against exceptionally inclement nature makes it yield more than what the U.S.S.R. with all its enormous natural resources can obtain by forced labour and shootings.

In the morning children rode to school on their bicycles. All were dressed in simple, sound clothes; all looked cheerful and well-fed.

The motor lorry in which we were travelling went at

the rate of about thirty-five miles an hour and did not break down once.

Afterwards we were put in a train; the carriage was clean and tidy, the passengers, looking calm and content, had respectable clothes and carried suit-cases.

In this 'capitalistic' country the carriages are of one class, sufficiently comfortable for all; in the 'socialistic' country across the frontier, decent carriages are only for the Soviet aristocracy and foreign visitors; those for ordinary people are filthy.

We were provided with bread, butter and sausage for the journey, and when the train stopped at some station where all the passengers were supposed to have a meal, unknown friends brought to our compartment a big parcel of sandwiches. We were runaways, still under arrest, and utterly defenceless, and yet we were travelling like ordinary passengers and our escort's sole concern was that we should have enough to eat.

'Well, they are an extraordinary people!' the boy said in surprise. 'They evidently have enough and to spare if they treat us to chicken sandwiches.'

Unfortunately, in Helsingfors I began by giving fresh trouble to everyone – I fell ill and had to be sent to a hospital. From the hospital stretcher I saw a bit of the town, clean as though it had only just been scrubbed, flowers in the front gardens, and shop windows with fruit of all countries and seasons.

I was not very keen on going to the hospital. When I was still rash and self-confident I used to say that I would not go of my own will either to prison or to a hospital. Since then I had had to spend in a hospital three weeks which seemed to me like three years. I was there looking after my boy who was operated on for septic appendicitis. He had to lie on an old straw mattress that was all bumps. There was one attendant to look after twenty-six children in the three surgical wards, and one sister in charge of the whole of the children's section. Soviet hospitals generally are so overcrowded that patients often die on the stairs because there are no beds and no room.

Dirty, ragged, blackened by the forest fire, the wind and the sun I felt ridiculously out of place in a room where everything was spotlessly white – walls, beds, tables, chairs and the nurses' starched bonnets, collars and aprons. But no one showed the slightest annoyance or surprise at my appearance!

A few minutes after I arrived I was put in the hands of the senior sister who took off my rags, gave me a bath, dressed me in clean things and put me to bed, doing it all so kindly and cheerfully, that one might think she enjoyed it. She covered me up with a white quilt and placed some flowers on the white table beside me.

I felt almost sorry that I was the only one to fall ill and that we were not all three in hospital.

Then they began asking whether I was hungry or thirsty. The substantial-looking senior sister in whose hands I felt like a baby mouse, said to me sternly in broken Russian:

'*Madame* wish or not, I run to kitchen.'

The kind woman would be surprised if she knew that in the country *madame* had escaped from, children in hospitals have even less to eat than at home.

In that hospital, which was the University clinic, I wrote most of this book, feeling as completely at peace with the world as though I had been born again.

Ingram Content Group UK Ltd.
Milton Keynes UK
UKHW022232190423
420461UK00005B/130